Mop

Deep Thoughts from a Shallow Mind

Dick Wolfsie

BLUE RIVER PRESS

Blue River Press
Indianapolis, Indiana

Mopey Dick: Deep Thoughts from a Shallow Mind

ISBN-13: 978-1-935628-09-5

Cover Design: David Finley
Layout: MaryKay Hruskocy Scott
Interior Illustrations Provided by: Paris Chrisopoulos
Proofreading and Editing: J. Heidi Newman

Printed in the United States of America
10 9 8 7 6 5 4 3 2 1

Blue River Press
Distributed by Cardinal Publishers Group
Tom Doherty Company, Inc.
www.cardinalpub.com

Introduction

Not a day goes by that something doesn't annoy or perplex me. My new washing machine has an 80-page manual I can't understand. The bank isn't happy with the passwords I want to use. I have 4,000 friends on Facebook I'd never heard of. I'm not allowed to get in my pajamas until 8 p.m. There's a gadget you can buy that scrambles an egg while it's still in the shell.

You probably share my frustrations, but you have had the decency to keep the whining to yourself. I'm sure you have also gotten locked in your garage naked or found your cellphone in the freezer. Okay, maybe I picked two bad examples.

By the way, whenever my wife and I are out in public, people tell her what a good sport she is for allowing me to make fun of her in my books. Mary Ellen has no idea what they are talking about. She thinks I'm a lawyer.

I hope you enjoy my rantings about daily life, but if you only read one book this year, please don't make it this one. I couldn't handle the pressure.

Table of Contents

MOPEY ABOUT MANHOOD

MOPEY ABOUT MONEY

MOPING ABOUT THE HOUSE

MOPEY ABOUT MEDIA AND MECHANICS

MOPEY ABOUT MARRIAGE

MOPEY ABOUT EVERYTHING ELSE

MOPEY ABOUT MANHOOD

Nude Breach

It was late Thursday night. I had gotten home after giving a speech in Covington, Indiana and I pulled into the garage about 11:00, tired and thirsty. The garage door closed behind me and I exited the car, entering the house. Mary Ellen was asleep and my son was in his room playing a video game.

I quietly went into the bedroom. I undressed, but before putting on my sleeping shorts, I decided to run downstairs first, let the dog out the back door for a few minutes and grab a small bottle of fruit juice from the garage fridge.

I retrieved the drink and turned the knob to re-enter the house. The knob refused to budge. "That can't be," I said to myself, "that door is always left unlocked. No way." And no clothes, either.

I panicked, banging on the door with both fists, bellowing Brett's and Mary Ellen's names. There was no response. Mark Twain must have been buck naked in his barn when he said: "Clothes make the man. Naked people have little or no influence on society."

Our bedroom door was closed; the ceiling fan was whirring. My son was in his room with headphones on, which was more than I had on. On a scale from one to ten, in order to be heard, I would need to make a disturbance that was a four. On the Richter scale.

My cell phone was in the car! I'd call the home phone and that would surely get someone's attention. It rang and rang but there was no answer. It went to voicemail. Out of habit, I left a message: "Hello, Mary Ellen. If you get this, I'm in the garage with no clothes on. When you have a moment, could you come downstairs and let me in?"

I hate to be a pessimist, but I didn't imagine she was going to check for messages at 11:30. Now what was I going to do?

The back door of the house was unlocked because I had let the dog out. All I had to do was sneak around and go through the entrance on the deck.

At that moment, I began to fully appreciate what my wife goes through when we plan an evening out. I needed to give some serious consideration to my wardrobe. What was appropriate for this occasion? I had two choices: A lovely 54-gallon black garbage bag or the 34-gallon clear plastic bags. I look terrible in black, but the other option seemed, well, redundant.

Instead, I opened the garage door and made my way along the side of the house; then as I neared the backyard, I bolted toward the deck, up the steps and into the living room.

The next morning I decided not to tell Mary Ellen what happened. I wasn't in the mood be made fun of. But I had forgotten about that voicemail. She called me from work later that day. "Dick, I just listened to the oddest message. Apparently, last night, about the time you were supposed to get home, there was a naked man in our garage. Now, who in heaven's name could that have possibly been?"

"I haven't the slightest idea, Mary Ellen."

I don't think she'll ever find out. I didn't leave my name in the voicemail.

Have a Heart

I take a heart stress test every two years. Back in 1990, they found a little plaque in one of my arteries, which surprised me because I floss almost every day.

I must admit, the staff is nice in the cardiac lab. That's like saying, "I didn't want to spend the night in jail, but I did meet some lovely people."

A stress test takes almost five hours. That gives you plenty of time to read *Prevention* magazine in the waiting room and wonder if you have any of the other 47 diseases they say you can avert if you just do all of those things you have no intention of ever doing.

I like blueberries and artichokes as much as the next guy, but they don't belong in a smoothie with tofu. I'd rather die. Which is the choice they seem to be giving me.

Protocol in the cardiac lab requires they explain the procedure every time. "By running on the machine, Mr. Wolfsie, we're going to try to increase your pulse and raise your blood pressure."

"What happens if that doesn't do it?"

"Then we whisper the cost of the procedure in your ear. That always does the trick."

Before I stepped onto the treadmill, I glanced up at a huge chart, 3 feet by 4 feet, an apparent motivation for me and others like me to mend our ways and adopt a healthier lifestyle. It was a multi-color depiction of three huge arteries, each representative of what havoc would be wrought if my blood were deficient in HDL, abundant in LDL or overflowing with triglycerides. In the graphic photo, each artery was clogged up, dripping with disgusting goo. It looked like an ad for Liquid Plumber.

“I don’t want to complain,” I said to the nurse during my last appointment, “but wouldn’t it be more soothing if you moved the treadmill in front of a window?”

“Mr. Wolfsie, this is a stress test, not 13 minutes at Club Med. Now start pumping those legs.” After 13 minutes, I was spent. I hadn’t walked that fast in two years and I was feeling the effects. I told the nurse I thought I needed the doctor.

“Oh dear, shall I call the cardiologist?”

“No, the orthopedist. My knees are killing me.”

When I was done with the treadmill, I was told I could relax for an hour before returning for the second part of the procedure. “Feel free to go to lunch if you’d like,” said the nurse. “And you may eat anything you want. There’s a Denny’s down the street.”

Then she shot a glance at the goopy arteries on the wall, flashed me a Cheshire cat grin and walked out of the room.

I walked into the Denny's. The waitress came over. "Can I take your order, Sir?"

"Yes, I'd like a garden salad with the low-fat vinaigrette dressing."

"Oh, you must have just come from the cardiac clinic. That place is just ruining our business. Please consider our Grand Slam: Three eggs, sausage, bacon and hash browns."

"Wow, do patients really order that?"

"Heavens no. But it's Dr. Morgan's absolute favorite."

After eating, I headed back to the lab. They took some photos of my heart and told me to come back in two years. I hope Dr. Morgan is still around. I'd love to go to breakfast with him.

Age Old Problem

I've been complaining lately about my poor knee that may require replacement, or at the very least, a little high-tech poking around by my orthopedist. I prefer the formal "orthopedist" to the alternative name orthopod, which sounds like I'm going to be strapped to a gurney and clawed by a lobster.

I have learned that my dog, Toby, has a virtually identical malady, a degenerating anterior cruciate ligament (ACL), making it difficult for him to negotiate stairs or chase squirrels. I stopped chasing rodents long ago, but I have no intention of sleeping downstairs on the couch with a chubby beagle.

It's bad enough that the two of us are starting to look alike, but I don't think we should be getting the same diseases. I still sprout an occasional pimple, but it would be hard to go to work with even a mild case of mange. And I can get a few days off if I get the flu, but I'm not going to call in sick with fleas. Not with my HMO.

Part of the problem is that Toby and I are the same age, assuming, of course, we observe the old canard that one year in a dog's life is the equivalent to seven in a human's. I don't think we do a comparable age adjustment with any other species.

"Hey, Charlie, how old is Fred, your giant turtle?"

"He's about a hundred and fifty years old—fifty-four in human years."

"Say, Neil, what's the age of that fruit fly of yours?"

"About eight seconds old. About 112 in human years."

Apparently your pet can get H1N1. I've had dogs and cats my whole life, and I've known that rabies was always a lurking possibility, but I never expected this. The article said that sneezing could be an indication of the virus in your furry friend, so I spent most of last week teaching Toby to sneeze into the crook of his right front leg. He was extremely resistant. I tried to get him to sanitize his paws with Puppy Purel, but he just stuck up his nose. You can't teach a dog good hygiene.

I am keeping an eye out for other symptoms. Chills are often present with the flu, but it's hard to tell if your pooch has the chills. When he is asleep, every part of his body ripples, so you don't know if he's having one of those erotic dreams about the toy poodle down the street or is possessed by an alien. It's tougher to see the signs with cats. Feline symptoms include lethargy and lack of interest in humans, which, correct me if I'm wrong, is the definition of a cat.

What do you do with a dog that has the flu? The experts recommend plenty of bed rest, which is easy since most dogs sleep about 18 hours a day. Millions of years ago, canines spent time hunting for prey, but now their food comes in a 40-pound sack, which I have to lug from the pet store, which is how I hurt my knee. This story is all starting to come together, isn't it?

I've tried strapping one of those masks on Toby's snout, but he keeps pulling it off and chewing it. I also have been insisting that he not have any nose-to-nose contact with any of his buddies, but that's been hard to enforce and, considering the alternative, I'm going to leave well enough alone.

Better Than This

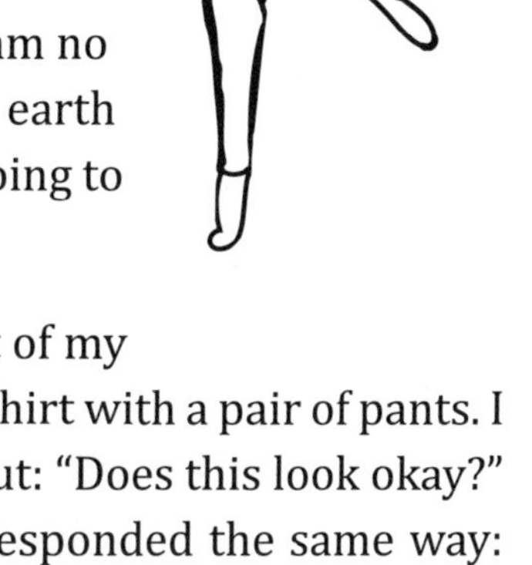

2012 marks my 30th year in television. It seems like just yesterday I was nervously standing in front of a camera, not sure which direction to look, unprepared for my segment, babbling away incoherently.

Wait a second. That *was* yesterday!

This insight has made me realize that there are countless things in my life I am no better at than when I started on this earth 64 years ago. I say countless, but I'm going to count some of them anyway.

1. Am I a better dresser? For most of my life, I've been trying to match a shirt with a pair of pants. I still ask my wife before we go out: "Does this look okay?" For our entire marriage she's responded the same way: "You look fine. Don't you have any other pants?"

2. Am I a better driver? I figure I've driven at least a million miles, but I still have half the world honking at me to get in my own lane. People still flip me the bird and shake their fist at me, much like the day I got my permit. Five decades—no improvement. Don't feel sorry for me. simply get the heck out of my way.

3. Am I a better golfer? Not by a single stroke. In fact, I'm worse. I've wasted 2,000 rounds of golf, 4,000 golf balls, 160,000 swings, and 10,000 expletives. I'm depressed simply writing about this. Of course, not enough to cancel

my tee time. I'm also no better in bowling. But here's the difference. I don't care.

4. Do I have a better sense of direction? When I was a toddler, I got lost in our two-bedroom ranch. I have gone to the same accountant for 30 years in the same office building. I still don't know which way to turn when I get out of the elevator.

5. Am I a better typist? I have written a slew of books, hundreds of newspaper columns and thousands of emails. I still have to look at the keys and I'd swear that the J keeps moving. Am I the only person who composes an entire email and when I finally look up before hitting "send," EVERYTHINJ IS IN CAPS?

6. Am I a better dancer? I have always done that gyrating thing where I snap my fingers and every once in a while I turn around. I still can't do that to the beat. I know I look absolutely ridiculous. The only reason people don't laugh at me is that they are looking at their own feet and doing the exact same thing.

7. Am I better at fixing things? Nope. I still hire a handyman to fix everything. All that has changed is the price. I now pay $50.00 an hour. If I offer to help, it's $60 an hour. Sometimes he'll say: "Why do you want to help me? What have I ever done to you?"

8. Am I better at making friends? I've always had two or three close friends. That has never changed. The friends keep changing, however. That should tell you something.

9. (This one is none of your business.)

10. Am I a better writer? Let's just say I'm glad you made it all the way to number 10.

Blood Work

Phlebotomists have a tough profession. Imagine having a job where everyone hates you for what you are about to do, and your first instruction to them is "make a fist."

My phlebotomist, Shirley, uses the same joke every time I see her. She looks at me with flirty eyes and says, "It's too bad you're married. You're my type." I laughed at this for about 11 of our sessions together, but now I have my own joke. When she tells me what a tough day she's had, I tell her to go with the flow. I'm not sure how much longer we can keep this up. Probably 'til my LDL goes down.

I try not to talk to people in the adjoining cubicles. You never know if there's someone there with a serious illness. I overheard a patient say his doctor told him he has obliterating arteriosclerosis and hypercholesterolemia. When we walked out together, I gave the guy a big hug and told him to hang in there and be brave. Then I went home and Googled what he said. We have the same thing.

And by the way . . . how long are you supposed to keep that silly cotton ball and bandage on your arm after you leave the doctor's office? I rip it off the second I walk out the door. My wife, who only gets a blood test once a year, tells the phlebotomist to take off the old bandage and stick her in the same place. She thinks if you remove the bandage, you jeopardize your health insurance coverage. This is the same woman who waits 20,000 miles to get her first oil change.

Shirley says that there are two kinds of people in the world: Those who watch when the needle goes in and those who don't. I asked her what kind of person would stare at the needle and she said they are usually up-tight, aging baby boomers who lead dull, uneventful lives and are control freaks. Ever since she mentioned that, just as she sticks me, I tell her what lovely eyes she has or how interesting the clinic ceiling is.

It makes me nervous when they put my blood in a vial and then identify it by simply putting my name on it with a magic marker. I'm not sure what else they could do, but that very same system failed in sleep-away camp 50 years ago and I ended up wearing someone else's underwear for four nights.

Shirley never sees my actual cholesterol numbers, but she gets a big kick out of the fact that I have to come back so she can stick it to me every three months. Sometimes she sneaks in a little medical advice of her own. Last week, she told me that Cheerios was good for raising my HDL. Or was it that Wheaties would help lower my LDL? Needless to say, she doesn't think much of Count Chocula.

When I left, Shirley had to do a final check of my personal information, so she took out a chart and pointed to various pieces of data with that same magic marker.

"Is that still your address, Mr. Wolfsie?"

"Yes."

"Is it still your phone number?"

"Sure is."

"And is that still your birth date, March 5, 1947?"

"Well, I'd love to change that to 1957." She smiled and made my suggested edit.

I walked out of the office on cloud nine. My cholesterol may still be sky high, but I feel 10 years younger.

Class Act

My 45th high school reunion was in 2010 in New Rochelle, New York, and while my generation was sipping Merlot, comparing Lipitor prices and kicking the legs on state-of-the-art walkers, I was vacationing in Egypt, looking at mummified people. Well, I walked myself right into that one, didn't I?

I felt bad about not seeing some of my old friends, but I'm not a huge fan of reunions. It's all very awkward. You're chatting with someone you haven't seen in 35 years when you spot an old buddy you haven't laid eyes on in 45 years who you liked better or played varsity baseball with or made out with in the back seat of your Chevy (and these last two were not the same person, in my case), and what are you supposed to do?

"Patty, I've enjoyed this 14-second conversation, but Aaron has showed up and he was in all my classes and we hung out together on weekends, and you were just in my homeroom sophomore year. And we only have two hours left in the reunion. There's always the 50th. How about one last hug?"

And so, I was okay with missing my 45th reunion. Then, a few months before the event, I got this email. It began: "New Rochelle High School is having a 40-year reunion. Please join us."

This was clearly a mistake, a typo or a wrong address. These things happen, especially with my classmates, few of whom could spell, many of whom cheated in typing by looking at their neighbors' keys. I continued reading. "We are trying to locate some of our teachers, so that they, too, can trip down memory lane with us."

Oh my goodness! This was not a reunion of my graduating class; it was the 40th reunion of the first high school class I taught back in 1969. "Trip" was the operative word, here. This was still the '60s, remember.

There was more . . . "Unfortunately we can't possibly treat every teacher who wishes to attend. If you cannot afford the $90, perhaps we can come up with a solution."

Was this a personal note to me? Had their reunion committee determined I had been unsuccessful in life when I left the classroom and probably needed some financial assistance? And they made it seem like there was an entire parade of teachers desperate to go to this reunion, which I kind of doubt. As I remember, most of the other faculty members had at least 30 years on me, so I think the pickins are going to be slim.

I read on. "If you would like to attend, and you are willing to pay $90, we would love for you to share this happy time with us. Our teachers helped make us who we are today."

I'll tell you what you are today: a bunch of cheap ingrates who won't lay out a lousy ninety bucks for the best teacher you ever had. Not only that, you guys always thought I was old, but I wasn't much older than you. And you probably think I became a grumpy old man. I don't think so.

I didn't go to the 40th for my ex students. If I wanted to see a bunch of senior citizens sitting around talking about their health, complaining about high food prices and lamenting how much better things used to be—heck, if I wanted that, I'd have gone to my own reunion.

Cramping My Style

I have leg cramps. I know the last thing you want to hear about are the medical problems of some two-bit humorist.

Actually, I've been surprised lately at how many people really do care about the fact that my calf locks up in a knot at night and the pain is so unbearable I feel like I'm giving birth to a Volkswagen.

When you're as old as I am, I think it's better to only have friends in your own age group. If I told a 30-year-old guy I had leg cramps, or shortness of breath, or was thinking of asking the doctor for those little blue pills, he'd shake his head, put the iPod back in his ears, jump in his Mini Cooper and take off.

I was in an elevator and a young man who had been a recent intern at WISH-TV was chatting with me. "So how have you been, Mr. Wolfsie?"

"Oh, okay I guess, but I do get these terrible leg cramps at night."

"Well, have a nice day. See ya."

On the way down in the elevator, I saw an old friend—a man of my own vintage. "Hey, Dick, how ya doin'?"

"Fine, Joel, except at night I do get these le . . . "

"Don't tell me . . . leg cramps. I used to get them also. Here's what I recommend: Take vitamin E three times a day. It's like a miracle."

I've never trusted the Internet for health information, but I am inclined to take advice in an elevator. To be sure, I did call my doctor to ask his opinion. He told me that vitamin E was not good for me because of an interaction with other medication I am taking for my cholesterol. Then he asked me exactly where I had gotten this faulty information. I told him the 14th floor of the Chase building. That's all he needed to know.

The next day, back on that same elevator, I ran into another old buddy—"old" being the key word here, again. "Hey, Dick, word is out you are having leg cramps."

"Wow, word sure travels up and down fast in this building."

"My dad had leg cramps and he drank a gin and tonic every night for 30 years before he went to bed—and he never had cramps again."

"What did it? The gin or the tonic?"

"Who cares? It worked."

I did some Googling and found that the gin helps you forget your pain, but it was probably the quinine in the tonic that really eased the cramps. For the next two weeks, I drank a quart of tonic before bed. It had little effect on the problem, so now I'm willing to at least consider the therapeutic benefit of gin.

Over the course of a month, I asked several friends, a few doctors and my good buddy Wendell Fowler, the nutritionist guru in Indy, about any possible remedies for my ailment. Here, in no particular order, are the cures that people swear by.

- Magnesium
- Zinc
- Vitamin E
- Turmeric
- Potassium
- Vitamin C
- Acupuncture
- Biofeedback
- Folic acid
- Calcium
- Fiber pills
- Cauliflower extract
- Yoga
- Black cherry extract
- Place a bar of soap under the fitted bedsheet

I am not going to take any of this advice, but I have noticed lately that my legs do tend to cramp at night on days when I have vigorously ridden my exercise bike. I'm no doctor, but I am prescribing to myself a complete lack of physical activity for the next six months and a shot of gin before going to bed.

I'd take it with tonic water, but I don't believe everything I hear in elevators.

Soap Suds

Newspaper writers know that most of their stuff ends up in the garbage along with the moldy cheese or in the recycle bin, assuming the reader is environmentally friendly. So it is always a real kick to learn that someone has cut out my column and stuck it up on the refrigerator next to their first grader's finger-painting or under a Rachel Ray recipe for chicken fricassee. That's about the most I could ask for.

The piece I wrote about my nighttime leg cramps resulted in the most emails I've ever gotten. In it I complained about this persistent problem, and mentioned that I had gotten a great deal of advice from people who also suffered from this malady. Suggestions included: Magnesium, Zinc, Vitamin E, Turmeric, Potassium, Vitamin C, Acupuncture, Biofeedback, Folic acid, Calcium, Quinine, Fiber pills, Cauliflower extract, and Yoga.

After the column appeared, I started getting emails that began like this:

"Dick, ever think of using soap?"

"Mr. Wolfsie, do you realize the importance of a bar of soap?"

"Hey, DW, a bar of soap can make a big difference in your life."

At first, I was mortified. I'm not a hygiene fanatic, but I don't think I missed a shower all last year—except that one morning I had to rush the dog to the vet when he swallowed a AAA Alkaline battery. I *was* a little sweaty in the waiting room, but if people are going to take a whiff of you during a crisis they shouldn't be judgmental.

All the emails contained a similar suggestion: to cure leg cramps sleep with a bar of soap in your bed. I was a bit cautious, of course. Maybe it was a grand conspiracy to tantalize me to do something really bizarre; then they could all laugh themselves silly about Dick Wolfsie at the office Christmas party, just at the mere prospect I may have fallen for it.

I showed these emails to my doctor that week. He said that he often recommended putting a bar of soap in the bed but hadn't mentioned it to me because he figured I already knew about it. Now, how would I know to put a bar of soap in my bed to cure cramps? Did I go to medical school like he did?

Anyway, that evening I tried it. I was hoping Mary Ellen wouldn't notice, because she's always accusing me of falling for every wacky idea out there.

"Dick, what's that strong soapy smell?

"Look, Mary Ellen, please don't think I'm totally nuts. And please don't think I'll believe every off-the-wall suggestion that people email me, but that odor is a bar of Dial soap that I placed in between the sheets of the bed."

"Well, I don't know why you'd do something so incredibly weird, but at least it might cure those leg cramps."

Forgotten Dreams

Whenever I pick up the newspaper, I find medical news contrary to something I had previously thought. And it's never good news.

Why couldn't they discover that those deep-fried Oreos are an excellent source of anti-oxidants and a possible preventative for heart disease. I know the news is coming, but please, I am begging the *New England Journal of Medicine* to release the research before the State Fair begins.

I read the other day that the sleeping pill I take may not be effective in getting me a better night's rest, but may, in fact, have an amnesia effect. In other words, I may be up all night pounding the pillows, tossing and turning, but when I awaken the next morning, I don't remember having trouble falling asleep. Just what I need: something else to keep me up all night.

The more I think about this, the crazier it makes me. The side effects of the drug include that some patients who take the prescription may sleepwalk, as well, which means I could be wandering throughout the house getting in all sorts of trouble, then in the morning not remembering anything.

I experienced this in college on occasion. You know, up all night cramming for a test, then not recalling a thing the next morning. (And I was drug free.)

Maybe it runs in the family. My younger brother used to be a sleepwalker. He'd get up in the middle of the night and grab a rod and reel from the garage, then walk out the front door at three in the morning. My mother wanted to call the doctor, but my father said we needed the fish.

I asked my wife if she had noticed anything odd over the past several weeks, anything out of the ordinary. "Well, I can't figure out why we're always out of cat food."

That scared the heck out of me. Especially since I've gained a few pounds over the past two months. "Anything else, Mary Ellen?"

"Well, let's see . . . I notice now in the morning that your bathroom is spotless. All your pill bottles are back in the cabinet. Your toothpaste tube has its cap on and all the towels are folded on the rack. Gee, maybe you are walking in your sleep."

"Mary Ellen, do you really think it's possible that I get up in the middle of the night and walk around the house but don't remember?"

"Of course, it's possible. You don't remember a lot of things."

"Like . . . ?"

"Like last week you thought you took the garbage out to the curb, but the stench from the garage said otherwise; you swore you had covered the lawn chairs before it rained, but that big wet area on the seat of your pants is evidence to the contrary. And you were 100 percent convinced you had watered my plants when I was out of town, but look at them."

"Oh, please, those flowers on the mantel look exactly the way they did the day you left."

"Yes, Dick, those are silk flowers."

Last night I decided to put sticky notes around the house so if I was sleepwalking, I could jot down what I did and maybe it would jog my memory. In the morning, I discovered that I had gotten into the fridge and polished off the remainder of my wife's homemade chicken cacciatore.

I'm glad I made a note of that. Sometimes I forget what a good cook she is.

Grumpy New Man

I have always wanted to be a grumpy old man. Over the years, I thought I had a made a lot of headway in this area, especially in the getting older part, which is easy. I also found myself getting progressively grumpier, as well. Or so I thought.

My father was a grumpy old man by the time he was 60 and I always admired my dad, so I aspired to be like him only sooner. Remember, 60 is the new 50. Or is it 50 is the new 60? Whatever.

I first tried to be a grumpy old man when I was in my 40s. Sadly, people mistook my crankiness for wittiness. I complained to the manager at Kroger that their entrance and exit doors were on the wrong side. "I'll never shop here again," I told him. "I don't know if I'm coming or going." That's pure old man stuff, don't you think? But did he call me grumpy? No, he burst out laughing—and told me I should use that line on TV.

In the '90s, my crabbiness got me nowhere. I once protested to a couple of Girl Scouts who came to the door selling cookies that their product was too high in fat and that eating S'mores would shoot my lipids through the roof. Their mothers called and thanked me, saying this was a good health lesson for seven-year-olds. Maybe I shouldn't have bought three boxes.

I did everything I could to acquire the label grumpy old man before my time. Nothing worked. I don't know how my dad did it with such ease. It must have been a gift.

Last year, I complained to some of my neighbors about their unkempt lawns. I fussed at others who were putting their garbage out at the curb two days early, and I put my foot down about kids making a ruckus shooting hoops on Sunday mornings when I was trying to sleep. This had codger written all over it. They made me president of the homeowners association.

I was starting to worry. When does one officially become a grumpy old man? I combed all my AARP magazines for a few hints, but their publication is more interested in readers avoiding this label than acquiring it. I called the periodical to grumble about their lack of coverage on this, and complained to one of the editors in the most crotchety way I knew how. "We welcome your feedback," she told me. "Please call again."

The problem here is that most people won't call you a grumpy old man to your face. They just think it.

"Did you get my email birthday card, Dick?" asked my friend David, a few days after my 60th.

"Yes, I did. Now, I must tell you, David, that I find email greeting cards rude. They lack the personal touch and it's annoying when I have to wait forever while they download."

"Why, you, you . . . "

"Go on David, say it. Please?"

"Okay, you . . . you probably have a good point. I should have taken the time to go to the store and buy you a nice Hallmark card, instead."

Even my best friends won't cooperate.

Maybe part of the problem here is that I don't have the right "look." I'm going to stop dying my hair and start hoisting my pants up to my ribcage. That will make a big difference.

I'm optimistic about my success. I'm not getting any younger, you know.

Height of Insult

I don't want to bore you with the health complaints of a 64-year-old. (When I became a sexagenarian, my wife thought Saturday nights were finally about to become more than dinner and a movie.) But my story begins with a medical scare and a series of doctor appointments. So many, in fact, that the phlebotomist at my internist's office started referring to me as "not you again," which is not the kind of greeting I was looking for at a lipid lab.

My symptoms, by the way, were visible pulsations in my lower legs. It looked like there were tiny aliens in my calf muscles trying to escape. I didn't go to the doctor at first because I kept dreaming that Sigourney Weaver was massaging my legs every night, so I wasn't looking for a miracle cure just yet.

In the course of the diagnostic process, I had to have my brain scanned. Like a cigar, they inserted me into a tube for an hour. During the procedure, I had a flashback to high school trigonometry class where I also stared at a blank ceiling listening to strange indecipherable sounds. At the hospital they give you a little buzzer to press if the experience becomes unbearable, a courtesy never afforded me by Mr. Lowenstein, my 12th grade math teacher.

A nurse called the next day to say that after examining my brain for 60 minutes, they were pleased to report they didn't find anything. I guess this was good news, but did the lab results have to be phrased quite that way?

Each doctor I visited required that I have my blood pressure, height and weight checked and rechecked.

I had never really paid any attention to my height. On my license, my passport and all medical questionnaires, I had always listed myself as 5-foot-10 inches tall—not as tall as my dad (a strapping six-footer) but taller than my mom, a petite 5-foot-3. I knew I was 5-foot-9 1/2, but I always rounded it up. I mean, who was I hurting?

"Okay," said one nurse after measuring my vitals, "blood pressure 123 over 80, height 5-foot-8, weight 175. Very good, Mr. Wolfsie, please step over here and . . .

"Whoa! How tall did you say I was?"

"That would be 5-feet, eight inches—in your socks, which adds a little, of course."

"Look, first of all, I'm 5-foot-10, maybe 5-foot-9 1/2, and second of all, these are expensive nylon socks, and very thin."

"Whatever you say, Mr. Wolfsie. Please grab one of the blue robes off that hook on the door . . . if you can reach it."

That night when I got home, I asked my wife how tall she thought I was. "Well, let's see, when I'm in heels, I'm taller than you, and I'm 5' 7", so I guess I'd say you are 5' 8". And you're still as about as cute and adorable as can be."

"But when we got married, I told you I was 5-foot-10.

"I figured you rounded it up from 5-foot-7.

And that's the end of the story. No life-threatening illness, but I'm either a pathological liar (misrepresenting my height for 60 years) and need some psychological counseling . . . or I am, and this is tough to admit, shrinking.

I haven't decided which one it is. It's going to depend on which one is covered by my medical insurance.

Mean Median

"Have you been drinking?" asked the officer, politely I might add, when he stopped me on Broad Ripple Avenue in Indianapolis, after I had turned west from Keystone. I was on my way home from a WISH-TV remote shoot, my usual Sunday morning beat.

"Drinking?" I said with a bit more hubris than is generally advisable when addressing a law enforcement officer. "It's 9:30 in the morning."

"When was the last time you had a drink?"

"I don't remember."

"That's not a good sign, Sir."

"That's not what I mean. I think I had a beer three nights ago," I stammered. Stammering, by the way, is not recommended during a situation like this.

The officer then explained that when I made my turn I "nicked the median with my front tire," and that in his experience as a police officer, "this usually means the person has had a few too many."

"Officer, this is silly. I'm not drunk. I'm just a lousy driver." As you can see, I was having trouble saying precisely what I wanted to say. Another bad sign, by the way.

The officer went back to his car with my registration. A few minutes later he returned to my vehicle. "May I ask if you have ever been arrested?"

"Arrested? Look, I know you're doing your job, officer, but other than three days overdue at Blockbuster, I've never been in trouble in my life."

"Sir, I am going to let you go, but based on your careless turn, I could give you a breathalyzer test to see if you are legally drunk."

"If it's legal, what's the problem?"

(Author's note: That last line I just made up. But the rest of the story is 100% true.)

When I got home, Mary Ellen asked me why I was so late. I told her that when I made a left turn off of Keystone I hit my front tire on the median and a cop pulled me over for being intoxicated.

"You do that all the time. Why didn't you just tell him you're a lousy driver?"

"I did tell him that."

Mary Ellen burst out laughing. "I was just kidding. I can't believe you said something that stupid."

The more I thought about this incident, the angrier I got. I called my friend Rob Butler, who sold me my car, and told him the story . . .

"That's amazing. How do these things happen to you?" asked Rob. "And the funny part is, you're a good driver."

"I am?"

Of course not, I was just kidding"

The more I thought about this faulty left-hand turn, the more I wondered about my driving ability. So I went back to that corner and made the same maneuver multiple times. In nine out of ten attempts, I was successful in negotiating that pesky strip that divides the street.

If I were a baseball player in the World Series, that would be a 900 average. But it wouldn't be for hitting. It would be for missing.

Movie Sadness

"One ticket, please."

"Just one?" asked the young lady. Then she looked at me like I was a lost puppy.

"Yes, just one."

I wish I hadn't emphasized the word "just." Suddenly I felt very self-conscious. It seemed like everyone was staring at me.

There were a few people milling about the theater lobby. An elderly couple smiled. I think they recognized me. Then I saw them whispering. Now I was paranoid. What were they saying? Maybe, "Oh dear, his wife must have left him. She probably read his last column." . . . "I always knew that humor was a solitary business, but there's nothing funny about being alone." . . . "Poor Dick Wolfsie. He apparently doesn't have a friend in the world."

Flashback to that morning. My wife had informed me that she wouldn't be home until late that evening. I had already

decided to spend the day at home to catch up on some work: write a few newspaper columns, prepare some speeches, maybe take a couple of two-hour naps.

That's when I decided not to blow the entire day. I'd go to the movies. True, I had never gone to a movie alone in my entire life. Really, how hard could it be?

Selecting a movie, for example, had always been easy. It usually went something like this: "Mary Ellen, let's go to the movies and see *The Social Network*."

"Oh, a movie's a great idea. How about we see *The Kings Speech* instead."

"Yes, dear." That was simple enough. Then I would pick a time. "Let's catch the 5 p.m., Mary Ellen. And get those matinee prices."

"No, let's go at 7 so I don't have to rush home from work."

"That works for me."

Deciding where to sit was always my decision. "Let sit up front, Mary Ellen."

"No, that's too close. We'll go in the middle."

"Okay, dear, but let's sit in the center of the row so I don't have to turn my neck."

"No, let's sit on the aisle, so it's easier for you to get me more popcorn."

But for this movie, I was without my consultant. So where to sit? There was only one other person watching *The Adjustment*

Bureau that afternoon and I did need someone to explain the movie to me. Plus, I felt sorry for the guy. He was all alone. When I sat down right next to him, he moved six rows down. So much for being friendly.

The film was okay, but I thought the storyline was a bit muddled. Maybe that's because when I returned from the men's room halfway through it, I walked into *Black Swan* instead.

I didn't get popcorn or a drink, because I forgot what size Mary Ellen tells me to buy. And I had trouble finding my car afterward because knowing where we parked has never been my responsibility.

When I arrived home, I decided to catch a little TV before Mary Ellen got back from her meeting. I figured that would help me forget how lost I had felt all day.

I'm glad she got home early. I couldn't find the remote.

My Achin' Back

I pulled into the parking lot, edged into a space by the side of the building, and carefully negotiated my exit from the car. My face was scrunched from the unbearable pain as I shuffled into my chiropractor's office.

I cautiously lowered myself into a chair in the waiting area. Now I had the dubious pleasure of perusing several charts of the skeletal system, each one a reminder of all the ways that any one of the 206 bones or 639 muscles in your body can turn on you and ruin a perfectly good weekend.

I tried to make conversation with a few other people who apparently were in great pain. "So, how did you hurt your back?" I asked one of the patients, a middle-aged man with a slight paunch.

"I'm a firefighter and I rescued a 300-pound man from a burning building. What happened to you?"

"I sneezed."

This caused quite a stir in the waiting room. The weightlifter was amused; so was the salt delivery guy. The two women from Fay and Fran's Piano Moving Company thought it was a hoot.

Everyone thought I was kidding. I wasn't. An explosive sneeze had done something wicked to my lower back and sent me crashing to the kitchen floor the day before.

The receptionist told me it was my turn to see Dr. Shepherd. He asked, "So what happened to your back, Dick? I heard you simply sneezed. Look, I have some very needy patients out in that waiting room."

"Well, you just heard part of the story, Doc. Yes, I sneezed, but it wasn't a normal sneeze. It was a sneeze of gargantuan proportions. Saving a guy from a burning building, delivering pianos, hoisting bags of salt . . . these are not the kind of stories you can slap together for an article in the *New England Journal of Medicine*. I'm the case history every chiropractor wants hobbling into his office."

He took an X-ray of my back, which he said was in pretty good shape considering I had 64,000 plus miles on my body, apparently a reference to my age. Coincidentally, my car also has 64,000 plus on it. To be fair, it's been in for service a lot more than I have. Although no one is offering me an extended warranty.

To lighten things up, the chiropractor asked if I had heard any good jokes lately. "Sure, here's a favorite, Doc. How many chiropractors does it take to change a light bulb? Only one, but it will take him seven visits to do it."

He didn't think that was at all funny, so I was concerned when he slapped pads on my back to send electric current though my body. It scared the bejeebers out of me when I peeked over my shoulder. I'd swear there were two witnesses and a priest watching the procedure from the other room.

After being jolted, I was adjusted, which meant the doctor folded me up in a little ball and smashed all 280 pounds of himself into my side. It actually felt good. And I know he thought this was a beneficial procedure because then he jumped on the adjacent table and said, "Okay, now it's my turn."

When I left his office, I did feel better. As I got into my car, I saw a frail old woman limping into the clinic. "This is my first time here," she declared. "Does the treatment work?"

I tried to be honest. "It's nothing to sneeze at."

No Bones About It

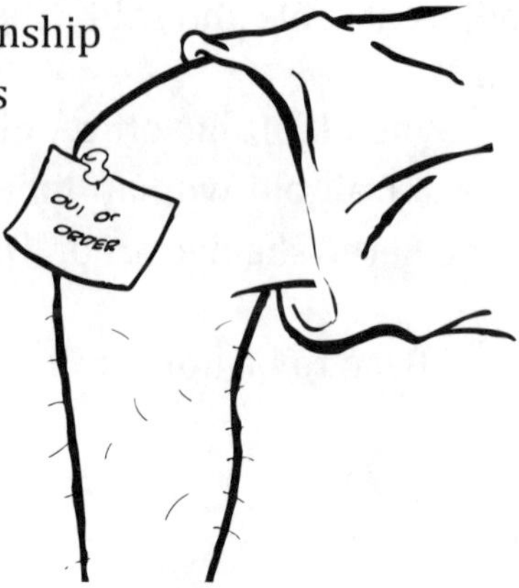

I've never had a good relationship with my left knee. Our problems together started back in college with a traumatic football injury. I was watching the homecoming game and my entire leg became wedged in the bleachers when I was trying to get a better look at one of the cheerleaders. Things have not been the same since.

Over the years, I have managed to remain relatively active, but I knew my knee was planning to retire way before the rest of me. For the last several months, I have felt like there was an entire family living inside my kneecap. I can hear a party going on inside, with lots of activity, clatter and a crackling fire. My wife asks me if it's the pain that keeps me awake at night. No, it's the noise.

After limping through most of the last year, I realized it was time to take some action so I made an appointment with an orthopedist. When I reached his office, I was greeted by an entire waiting room of people who were there to make a trade. Everyone sitting near me was having something replaced—a knee, a shoulder, an elbow. One guy confused his metatarsal with his Taurus and thought he was at a Cash for Clunkers event.

During my appointment, the doctor fumbled around with my leg, contorting it in several directions, and then asking me if it hurt. Funny, because when I'm lounging on the sofa watching *Dancing with the Stars* I'm in agony, so you can imagine how my calf felt when it was twisted into a pretzel.

The doctor told me he needed to get some "pictures" of my knees, which was embarrassing since all I had handy were three snapshots of me in a pair of ugly green Bermuda shorts.

I went to an imaging center for an MRI. The receptionist showed me a stick outline of a guy and asked me to put an X over the knee that was troubling me. This was difficult because I was looking at a figure looking at me, so his right was my left. It was way too complicated, so I simply pulled down my pants and drew an X on my own knee. The nurse said not to do this because doctors are never sure if X marks the spot to operate or *not* to operate. Also, I was still in the waiting room.

When I left, the nurse handed me a huge envelope of images to bring back to my doctor—about 64 of them, more pictures than we have of our wedding.

That night I glanced at the radiologist's report. It was the scariest thing I ever read in my life. *Within the intercondylar notch region posteriorly . . . there is an irregular structure . . . consistent with a loose body.* Okay, I'm no doctor, but that sounds like they're saying I have something wrong with my butt.

And this:

There is a tearing of the anterior horn and the posterior horn, near the meniscal root.

I think this is what happened in my high school parking lot 45 years ago after the bus ran over the band equipment.

When I went back to the doctor, he said my bad knee was 62 years old and that was the simplest explanation he could give me.

I told him my good knee was also 64 years old. Just for future reference, it's tough to make an orthopedist laugh.

Now Hear This

I never know quite how to behave when I go to the doctor's.

I once had the giggles during a blood draw, and several years ago when they ripped the EKG pads off my hairy chest, I said a bad word. Generally, I bend over backward not to draw attention to myself, although one other time I was bending over forward and I may have yelped.

For my most recent annual check-up, I was sitting in the waiting room filling out a new form that asks if you have contracted any new diseases since your last appointment. Maybe I'm old school, but if I had developed something serious, I probably would have squeezed in another visit.

The last page of the questionnaire was a survey titled: A SIMPLE TEST TO SEE IF YOU HAVE A HEARING LOSS. This was in big, bold capital letters, like they were already yelling at me—as if hard of hearing is closely connected to hard of reading.

The survey had 10 questions to diagnose the problem. Here they are, verbatim:

1. *Do others complain that you watch TV with the volume too high?*
   Every night, my wife comes into the bedroom while I'm watching Leno, looks at me and says, "I can't believe how loud this is." I know she is saying that because I can read lips.

2. *Do you frequently ask others to repeat themselves?* Constantly. "Say that again," I'll yell at a friend at lunch. You would, too, if you heard some of the crapola people believe after watching cable news.

3. *Do you have to sit up front in church to understand the sermon?* First of all, I'm Jewish. When I was a kid in religious school, I cut my Hebrew class all the time. Even when my hearing was perfect, I still did not have a clue what the rabbi was talking about.

4. *Do you have difficulty understanding women?* The questionnaire says some loss is so gradual, you don't really know you have a problem unless someone brings it to your attention. Gee, I wonder who that would be?

5. *Do you have trouble understanding children?* Babies? Not a word. Toddlers? Not a problem. Teenagers? Not a clue.

6. *Do you know where sounds come from?* This is a tricky one, like the 'tree falling in the forest' question. Here's another: If your spouse is complaining about something and you can't hear the griping, is there still a problem?

7. *Can you hear people in another room?* No. That is the major reason I went into another room in the first place.

8. *Have others mentioned that you don't seem to hear them?* Maybe, but I think I was in another room at the time.

9. *Do you avoid family meetings because you can't understand the conversations?*
   No, I avoid family meetings because in the words of Hoosier humorist Kin Hubbard: There is plenty of peace in a home where the family doesn't make the mistake of trying to get together.

10. *Do you have ringing in your ears?*
    Yes, so I answer the door. Sometimes there's no one there. But on TV, somebody has company.

Being a little hard of hearing has worked to my advantage. The other day my wife came to the basement while I was installing a new printer. She asked: "What kind is it?"

"It's about 8:30," I told her.

That's an old joke. But my wife hadn't heard it.

Pain in the Foot

If you dream you have foot cramps and the pain wakes you up, but then it's gone when you open your eyes, do you really have foot cramps?

This is the great philosophical question I am going to tackle because I have given up on that troublesome one about the tree falling in the forest, which has kept me tossing and turning for several decades.

I hate those brain teaser things you see in books and magazines. Things like: If I lie about everything, am I telling the truth now? When I read these kinds of teasers I want to find the person who came up with such an inane question and put him out of my misery.

A few years back, I was having nightly leg cramps, which constantly woke me. I couldn't go back to sleep so I spent the wee hours of the morning massaging my legs, wrapping them in hot towels and popping magnesium pills. Ah, those were the good old days. Now things have gotten complicated and out of my reach. This time it's my feet.

When I woke up the other morning my wife asked me: "So, how did you sleep?"

"Not well. Foot cramps woke me up several times. I had them all night. It's hard to believe I slept at all."

"What did you do to stop them?"

"I didn't have to do anything. Once I opened my eyes, the cramps were gone, so I went back to sleep."

"Well, maybe you dreamt you had them?"

"Please don't say things like that to me, Mary Ellen. You know stuff like that keeps me awake."

"Bingo, you're cured! You'll never have foot cramps again. What would you do without me? By the way, will never sleeping again make you even grumpier than you already are?"

Each of the next three nights, I was awakened again. Throbbing, piercing foot pain. I bolted straight up in bed. "What's the matter, Dick? Foot cramps again?"

"Yes, but I swear I wasn't dreaming… although, I am surprised to find you sleeping next to me. Where's Charlize Theron?"

I finally called the doctor and explained the problem. My discussion with him made things much worse. "Dick, are you still taking that mild sleeping pill I prescribed?"

"Yes, why?"

"The cramps may be a side effect of the sleeping pill."

"So, I'm not just dreaming I have cramps?"

"I'm not sure, but I'd stop taking the pill for a few weeks and see what happens."

"But my wife says if I don't get a good night's rest, I'm sleepy and grumpy and sometimes dopey. What do you think, Doc? What am I missing, here?"

"I think there are three more dwarfs."

I'm not quite sure what to do, now. The doctor thinks I'm crazy, my wife says I'm a hypochondriac and Charlize won't take my calls. The good news is that maybe I'm really asleep when I start to think I have thinning hair, arthritis, bad knees and worsening eyesight. Perhaps this is nothing more than my active imagination working overtime while I slumber.

I can dream, can't I?

Picture of Health

A neuroscientist at the University of California posts photos of everything he eats on his Facebook page. The expression "feed your face" has taken on a new meaning. This professor claims that revealing your food choices to the world will motivate you to eat better.

According to Dr. Garcia, he includes daytime snacks, late-night raids of the fridge, even the doughnuts he hid under the front seat of his car. He claims he has uploaded 9,000 pictures onto his Mac, which included a few dozen Big Macs, I might add.

I'm not sure this is a totally new idea. Unlike the good doctor, I've been uploading meals and then downloading them onto my dress shirts for more than 60 years. It is not uncommon for people to ask me about certain food choices I have posted on my clothing for all my friends to see . . .

"Looks delicious, Dick. Wasn't that the special at the Olive Garden last week?"

"Been to a ball game, Dick? I recognize the mustard."

People are always imposing a visual record of their lives on others. I am tired of friends showing me their pets on their cell phones. In fact, I'd rather see a serving of French fries than a French poodle. An adorable pic of your granddaughter on her new trike isn't very interesting to me. Show me a snapshot of a slab of smoky babybacks and I'd be happy to say: "Awww, how cute."

My concern is that publicly sharing your food intake encourages cheating. You may have read, for example, how much dishonesty there is with online dating. Men and women fudge their age, for example. Talking about fudge, what's to stop a woman from taking the Hershey bar she ate for lunch and with some Photoshop magic, turning it into a little plastic bag filled with baby carrots? Men are more deceiving. Sure, it looks like a $45.00 rib-eye from St. Elmo, but it's really a cheap piece of beef off the grill at Golden Corral. With men, always be wary of digital enhancements.

The other problem is that you leave your entire culinary life open to wicked rebuke from the masses. If you think Bruno of *Dancing with the Stars* would be tough on your Cha Cha, wait 'til he critiques that Chimichanga you inhaled for breakfast.

I eat a lot of meals in the car so this would also create a bit of an inconvenience for me and jeopardize my already questionable driving record.

"Did I do something wrong, officer?"

"You suddenly pulled off onto the I-70 shoulder. Is everything okay?

"I'm taking a photo of my fish sandwich."

"Sir, this time I'm only going to issue a warning: Those are really high in sodium."

Restaurants might try to benefit from this obsession with food photos. They already put little icons next to menu choices, so we'll know which items are low in fat. Now we'll also know which ones are high in resolution. The waitress will not only ask if you have room for dessert, but whether you have enough disc space. Is the meal dietetic? Who cares, as long as it's photogenic.

Personally, I don't think posting your meal choices on Facebook will catch on, especially in Indiana. Hoosiers are good people with high moral standards. They don't want their kids looking at corn all day on the Internet.

Weighty Decision

My wife casually mentioned to me the other night that I had a pathetic looking chest. While I suppose your better half is permitted to assess your upper half, I'd suggest not responding in kind. She thinks my body lacks definition, but I disagree. You can look it up in the dictionary under scrawny. Women are definitely more interested in men having muscles than a sense of humor. No female has never said: "I wish Matthew McConaughey would put his shirt back on and tell more jokes."

I used to go to a gym to play racquetball, and I'd see men and women fine-tuning their physiques, yet I wasn't inspired to fiddle with my own. Never really interested in the pure pursuit of brute strength, I would watch weightlifters during their routine. They'd pick up a heavy thing, then they'd put it down again. Such indecision.

After this stinging critique of my body, I read in *Prevention* magazine that when you reach 45 years of age, you begin losing one percent of your bone density and muscle mass every year. Old photos of me from high school show there was very little mass to start with, although some did roll in across my midsection in the early '80s. Density? I asked Mary Ellen about that, but she said not to worry, that I'm as dense as I've ever been—and she's not one to toss out compliments.

I was embarrassed into starting a moderate body-building regimen. I don't go to the gym to work out, however. I do everything at home, in the reclining position, while watching cable news in the evening. Why didn't I think of this 15 years ago? I still wouldn't like Sean Hannity, but at least I'd be buff enough to throw king-size pillows at the TV from a prone position. Some of my other favorite moves are curls, extensions and squats. There are two techniques I don't perform: abductions and snatches. I don't need any more legal trouble after getting caught walking out of Dick's Sporting Goods with a set of free weights. Hey, that's what the sign said.

I'm making progress. Thursday I "bed-pressed" a hefty amount: 18,000 grams. It sounds impressive when counted the way the British do. I took one really heavy dumbbell and managed to hoist it over my head. When I put it down, the dog scooped it up in his mouth and buried it outside.

Mary Ellen, who regularly works out with a trainer, says my new resolution to lift things is a good sign. She's hoping it will carry over to lifting a finger around the house to help. Or picking up the check when her brother and sister-in-law come to visit. As for me, this has all helped lift my spirits. I can now hold a six-pack out in front of me, arms parallel to the ground, for an entire TV commercial.

A few days ago, one of my macho neighbors helped me lug a huge barbell up to the second floor of our house. My hope was that after a few months working out with some of the lighter weights, I would one day be able to lift this new behemoth all by myself. Mary Ellen thought it looked ugly in our bedroom. So she took it down to the basement.

What a Racquet

I'm at the very bottom. Lower than . . . well, you know the expression.

I guess someone has to be last on my club's racquetball ladder, a members-only online display of the win-loss record of players and their scores. I'm not ashamed of my feeble ranking. If it were that big a deal, WikiLeaks would be all over it.

I first stated playing back in the '70s. Racquets were smaller then, but my ego was larger. I cared about every victory. Now that I'm too old to win, I think it's unseemly to be so competitive. Am I the picture of mental health, or what?

I once thought this was a relatively easy game because how bad do you have to be to miss an entire wall? And you have four walls you can aim at. Plus a ceiling. Some courts have a back wall made of glass so the health club members pumping up their enviable biceps can chuckle as they watch me play. The men laugh at me, too.

I'm always looking for a game, but not with just anyone. I'm quite selective since I know I'm going to be dominated, so I want an understanding partner. I send out emails looking for some action. "D player looking for another D. An A-C relationship is out of my league. But I am comfortable with a D-C pairing." Racquetball players are real swingers.

The other day while trying to bend over and tie my shoes, I noticed some men on the next court. One guy had all the moves. Oh, he was definitely a player although he was a little overweight. But that's my type. I feel I have a better chance because the competition isn't as great with the other singles. I decided to call him and see if he was interested in a match. He said he had a partner he was committed to but would be willing to get together for something extra, if we could meet early on Tuesday mornings. We played for a few weeks, but it never got serious. (I always end up a loser in these relationships.)

Technically, there's no real disadvantage to playing racquetball when you're older. Of course, you're not as fast on your feet and you don't think as quickly as you used to. You also have to stop after every game to visit the john. And people are always asking, "Are you okay?" like they've never heard anyone wheezing before. Oh, and you can't remember your locker combination.

I've had some memorable low points in my racquetball career, both on live television. In 1995, Sudsy Monchik, the number one player in the country, crushed me 15-6. A respectable outcome, I thought, except that he was using a four-pound cast iron frying pan instead of a racquet. I also lost to my good friend Gary Baker who had just returned from Barcelona where he finished number two in the world competition . . . for disabled athletes in wheelchairs. Both of those are true stories.

I do love the game and will continue playing despite what my knees are trying to tell me. Every time I lose to younger guys, they say I did great considering how old I am. The older guys whip me, they say I have potential. I can use that kind of encouragement, which is why I won't play anyone my own age.

MOPEY ABOUT MONEY

Dollar for Your Thoughts

Some relationships are so fulfilling and so beneficial to both parties that the end is tough to deal with when it's inevitable. But, I have to accept the fact that it's over.

The Dollar Store near me is closing. Forever.

I wrote about this store a couple of years ago and admitted my addiction. My house is filled with humongous bags of popcorn, dozens of bottles of generic root beer, tiny tins of anchovies and fourteen sets of Phillips head screwdrivers.

I am not ignorant about the pitfalls of addiction. My concern had always been that if this store ever closed, would I be able to handle it? Could I keep my world from crashing in on me? As a true junk junkie, I knew that when the supply of cheap product dwindled on the street, I would go through an excruciating withdrawal.

That was the good thing about the Dollar Store. Withdrawal was the smallest of your problems. In fact, a small withdrawal of $30.00 from the ATM got me all the laundry baskets, pickled okra, gift wrap, and power steering fluid that I would need for a week.

I am not a stranger to addiction. When I broke my Twinkie habit many years ago, I nibbled on Yodels and Snowballs during the transition, just to prevent sweating and the shakes. But there is no step-down program for the Dollar Store. Heroin addicts find some relief with methadone as a substitute, but there is no Dollar-Fifty Store—no halfway haven between dollar nirvana and paying three bucks for barbeque potato chips.

Some people yearn for closure. I dread it. Last year Donatos Pizza inexplicably closed up shop just down the block from me. They took their pizza dough and marinara sauce and had the crust to move elsewhere. I dabbled in Dominos and partied with Pizza Hut for a while. It wasn't the same. But I managed.

Several years ago, Breugger's, a bagel chain out of Pennsylvania, opened for business in town. It closed less than a year later, which was sad because Breugger's offered a real New York bagel. I had to go cold turkey. I also went corned beef and roast beef. But I had to do it at Panera and Einstein's.

My bank never went out of business, I don't think, but they did keep changing their name like an uncle of mine who was on the lam from the IRS. First it was AFNB, then it was Bank One and now it's Chase. I think they should make up their minds, but I have made the transitions pretty effortlessly. I think Bank One had crisper bills, but it all spent the same. I thought about going to Fifth Third. Of all the banks that should have changed names, that was the one. Would you keep your money in a financial institution that can't reduce a fraction?

But the Dollar Store closing is different. There are other dollar stores, but I knew this one like the back of my hand. I knew where the apple juice was and the ginger snaps. I could put my finger on the cheap shampoo and nobody knew no-name frosted flakes like me.

I'll miss the place. I do have a great idea for what they could put there instead. A hundred pennies for my thoughts?

Current Losses

I have been following my wife around our house recently. And she's been following me. At some very unpredictable times, in some very unlikely places, I find myself alone with Mary Ellen in a dimly lit room.

The other night, I was burning the midnight oil in my home office, working on an essay. My wife snuck into the room, looked into my eyes and said, "I don't think we'll be needing this." With that, she clicked off the overhead light, leaving only the glow of my desk lamp to illuminate her lovely face.

You probably think this is downright adorable, how the interest can still be there after so many years together. I recommend that every couple try this, no matter the stage of—or how long you have endured—your marriage. The Wolfsies have certainly benefited. In fact, we can measure our success.

Why, last month alone, by not leaving on unnecessary lights, we saved $13.45 in electricity.

This is part of my wife's obsession with going on a budget, which first reared its ugly dread last December. Christmas morning, I was surprised when I eyed my pile of gifts, and it was a bit more plentiful than my wife's. I was prematurely joyful. I opened one of the most enticing packages.

"Ooo-kay . . . this is a library book, isn't it?" I asked, trying to hide a tinge of disappointment.

"I know! Isn't that a great idea for a present, Dick? Instead of blowing 30 bucks on a bestseller—which you do every week—or buying expensive CDs online, I picked a few classics at the library, wrapped them up and stuck on a bow. Are you surprised?"

"Shocked, really. I forgot I was a Nathaniel Hawthorne fan."

"And that really huge package over there? Guess what it is."

"Well, I always wanted a Mini Cooper. But I have a feeling it's the complete works of James Fenimore Cooper."

"Aw, you peeked. I hope you enjoy your gifts."

"Of course, Mary Ellen, but like every other year, I'm going to have to return everything you gave me."

"Okay, Dick. Now let's each name something else we think the other person could save on. For example, I think you should give up that cup of java and apple turnover you've picked up every day on the way to work for 20 years."

"Why would I do that?"

"According to an article I read in Fortune magazine, if we had saved that five bucks a day for 10 years, invested it in Google, then sold all that stock before October of 2000, we'd be millionaires. I bet that puts a little crimp in your caffeine addiction."

"Just think: if I had been going to Starbucks instead of Speedway, we'd be billionaires."

"Here's another way we can save, Dick. Beginning today, we are going to start to make sacrifices. We could save by changing the oil in the car ourselves; we could save by doing the lawn work ourselves; we could save by cleaning out the gutters ourselves; and we could save by washing the car ourselves. I certainly hope you know the meaning of the word 'save.'"

"Mary Ellen, I also hope you know the meaning of the word 'we.'"

My Life Saving

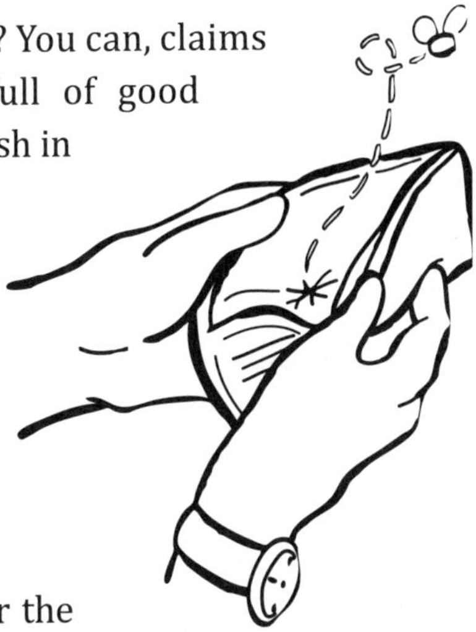

Would you like to save $14,450? You can, claims the Entertainment book, chock-full of good deals, brimming with coupons, awash in discounts. For a cheap person like me, it's my savior.

My wife advised me not to pay $25.00 for the annual publication. She claimed we'd never use the coupons—and if we did, we'd either go on the wrong night, end up at the wrong place, or the coupon would have expired. I consider this user error and decided that with proper management of my discounts, the result would be monumental savings.

A few months ago I said, "Here's the plan, Mary Ellen. For the next few months we are going to try to go to every place in this book, all 569 of them. Think of the money we'll save. Think of the fun we'll have. It will be like a second honeymoon, only this time we'll get two one-topping pizzas for the price of one . . . as long as we buy a liter of Pepsi and we don't have it delivered."

With that, I laid out on the kitchen table an elaborate chart detailing the itinerary—our cost-saving journey through Central Indiana. My wife was not impressed. "I don't mind dinner at the DQ, but do we have to play a game of Laser Tag the same night?"

"First of all, it's not *one* game, it's two. So don't poop out on me. It's the second game that's free."

"According to this, Dick, you also want to get up early Sunday morning and go duck pin bowling."

"Do I know how to plan a vacation, or what?"

"I do think we'll be tuckered out from the two hours of paintball on Saturday night."

Mary Ellen had a point. The first couple of weeks were exhausting. Morgan's River Rentals in Brookville may have been an especially bad choice. To get the discount you had to rent two boats, and I think we'd have had more fun and been less tired if we were in the same canoe.

We were like kids: trampolining, wall climbing, go-karting and miniature golfing. It was a little disconcerting watching Mary Ellen swing at 100 mph fast balls, but what else are you supposed to do with 50 free tokens at a batting cage?

When it came to dining, we had hundreds of restaurants to choose from. Most were fast food locations. Mary Ellen was burgered out. "Didn't we already eat at White Castle four times this week?"

"We still have six coupons left for sliders."

"But, Dick, it's nine o'clock in the morning."

"I know, that's why the line is so long."

We did have some relaxing days: two for one at the Muncie Children's Museum, the Basketball Hall of Fame Museum, and the Indianapolis Zoo. At the aquarium in Newport, Kentucky, we were offered a free kid's ticket if we bought two adult tickets. The problem was, we forgot to bring a kid. Later that day, we also got three Big Macs for the price of two. One of them is still in the glove compartment.

Overall, we had a great summer. We saved about $1,200. And it only cost us $3,000.

Round Figures

I think it was a perfectly reasonable thing to do. Knowing we had to board our dog during our two-week vacation last year, I stopped by the Lucky Dog Daycare Center every Monday for two months and gave them $20.00 to add to my account.

"That is so dumb," said Mary Ellen. "Why would you do that?"

"It's hard to explain. I didn't miss the twenty dollars, but if I had to write a check for $450 when we got back from the trip, it would have really seemed like a lot of money."

"But, Dick, you didn't save any of that money, you just dribbled it out over two months."

With that, I thought there was some glimmer of hope that Mary Ellen understood. She did seem to grasp the dribble concept. She did forget, however, what a habitual pre-payer, rounder-upper, and rounder-offer I am. What's sad is that I was getting away with this for my entire 30-year marriage (well, it's more than that, but some numbers you round down)—until the dreaded doggy daycare incident.

When I get an electric bill for $87.45, I send them $100. Why? First because I like those even numbers in my checkbook, and second because the next month my bill will be about $13.00 less. And if I keep doing this for about nine months, all of a sudden I get a month free from IPL. They have no idea I'm putting something over on them.

This obsession goes way back. When I first started driving in the '60s, I always put exactly five dollars' worth of gas in the tank. Later it was ten dollars. Then 20, 30, 40 . . . now 50. Never $50.13. See, this is starting to make sense, isn't it?

Oh, it gets worse. Please don't tell my wife. I figured that after paying for our cruise, we'd still have about two grand in expenses during the trip so I pre-paid the Visa card before we left. Why? So it would seem like we got everything in Hawaii for free. Isn't it obvious? There must be one person in (fill in your county) County who comprehends this.

Okay, I know what's happening now. In half the homes, someone is saying something like: "Hey, Gladys, listen to this. Dick Wolfsie does the same thing I do. I'm not alone in the world. Now get off my case."

In the other half: "Herb, Dick Wolfsie is loonier than we ever thought. You have to read this to believe it. His wife must be a saint."

Of course I wish I had never mentioned this to Mary Ellen because now she's on the lookout for any misbehavior. When the water bill is $37.18, she wants me to write a check for exactly $37.18. How incredibly weird is that?

Oh, and as I write this essay, it's 10 p.m. on a Tuesday. To me, that's close enough to call it Wednesday. I've tried to explain this thinking to Mary Ellen a million times. Wives never understand, do they?

Well, that's it for this report. I'm supposed to make this into a three-minute essay for my WFYI radio segment.. This one is about 2 minutes and 30 seconds . . .

In my world, I'm good to go.

The Seven Percent Solution

I believe in change as much as the next person. I believe in change so much that I have an old pickle jar in my home office filled with quarters, nickels, dimes and pennies. Also some golf tees, safety pins and wintergreen Lifesavers.

When I was a kid, I saved the exact same way. After a few months, I'd pour the stash in my pocket and jangle my way down to the store, or I'd ask the bank for some wrappers in assorted colors and carefully count out the 40 quarters or the 50 dimes required to fill the roll.

The thrill of this incremental savings technique never wore off for me. Well, not until recently. That container in my office held a nice nest egg. I took the sealed jar into my bank, hugging it tightly. I assumed the friendly teller would toss my hard-earned change into a high-tech coin counter, then sweeten my bank account with this windfall. Instead, I got the bad news . . .

"Mr. Wolfsie, we can count this for you, but we'll have to subtract 7 percent from your deposit for administrative costs and wear and tear on our counting machine."

"Wait a second. You're going to charge customers to put money into your bank?

Are people that dumb?"

"Apparently. That's why it's called chump change."

I told my wife about the problem and she suggested that I have Brett, our son, count the money and we'd give him 4 percent of the total, a savings of several dollars over the bank's fee.

"Gee, Mary Ellen, that's a brilliant idea. Then we'll know exactly how much money we owe Brett, but what will we do with a two-gallon jar of sorted quarters, nickels, dimes and pennies?"

"We'll deposit the rolls in the bank."

"Don't you get it? They don't care about our calculation. They have to add it up themselves in that cockamamie machine. They're not going to take Brett's word for it."

"Well, they don't know what an honest young man he is, do they? Maybe you should introduce him. Did you mention he took calculus in college?

At this point, I dumped the money on the carpet, and starting adding it all up. An hour later I'd calculated a total of $432.50. Now I knew exactly how much change I had, and I was in the identical predicament I was in before I counted it.

One option was to use the Coinstar machine at the supermarket. They charge 9 percent but you get all your money back if you take it in the form of a gift certificate to a restaurant. Sorry, but after a year of watching that nest egg grow, I was looking forward turning that into a romantic meal and a fine bottle of wine, not 22 fried catfish specials at MCL.

Then, I wondered if I could sell the money on craigslist or eBay. How would I word the ad?

> $432.50 for sale. $410.00 or best offer.*
> Fair condition, some scratches and smudges.
> Hand counted.
> * Cash only

I was still convinced that some bank out there would count my change without a fee, so I spent the better part of one afternoon investigating several branches. I finally got home and told my wife that it was a lost cause and that I was tired of toting around a 20-pound jar of coins.

And to make matters worse, I got a parking ticket. The meter had expired.

Don't Bank on Privacy

What is the name of your favorite cartoon character?

Are you teetering between Bart Simpson and Barney Rubble? If you are from my generation you might be torn between Bugs Bunny and Daffy Duck.

This was exactly the dilemma I faced recently when trying to create a security profile to do online banking. The bank asked me a series of personal questions so that if I forgot my password, they could confirm my identity by matching my answers.

Because the questions are so about me, the idea is that I won't have to scribble my responses in black marker on the side of my printer where I already store dozens of secret passwords. Then if I want to check my balances at 3:00 in the morning after a bout with insomnia or a six pack of Bud Lite, I can enter my code incorrectly up to three times, but they'll still allow access if I can remember five of the following:

My most unique characteristic? I seem to vacillate between feeling unbelievably funny and romantically dashing. On a bad day, I'd have to go with incredibly annoying. That only gives me a one out of three chance of getting that right. This all depends on what day I forget my password. Better not use that one.

Who is your favorite fictional character? You must be kidding. I couldn't answer that question on my final exam in American Literature. Okay, how about Moby Dick? Wait, they might not accept animals. Okay, just to look smart I'm going to say King Lear. But I know if get asked this under pressure after midnight, I'm going to end up saying Bugs Bunny again.

What is your favorite flower? I don't have a favorite flower. I have never had a favorite flower. If I indicate rose, there's a good chance I'd say chrysanthemum the next time. Well, maybe not. I don't know how to spell it. No bank balance for me.

What was your favorite gift as a child? Who could forget that Lionel train, Christmas 1956? Or that BB gun when I turned 13? Wait a second, that erector set was really cool. And I still have my Lincoln Logs. No, I'd never remember the right answer to that one.

Where did you go on your honeymoon? Out West. Somewhere in California. It's been 27 years. Give me a break.

Who was your first girlfriend? I'm going to say it was my wife, Mary Ellen. That's not true, of course, but if I said Cindy, Ginny, Marcia, Gale, Janet, Bonnie or Alice, she'd never let me forget it. But I would forget it. Which means I can't pay my bills online because I can't remember my password.

Who is your best friend? Well, right now I don't have a best friend because lately everyone has really ticked me off. And I'm not so quick to list someone as a best friend when for all I know that person has not named me as his best friend. Not that I'm petty.

What college did you apply to but not attend? Well, that would be all the colleges that rejected me, so let's see: Syracuse, Northwestern, Boston University, Brown . . .

This is embarrassing. Thanks anyway—I'd rather be overdrawn.

MOPING ABOUT THE HOUSE

Wishy Washy

From the beginning of our relationship, my wife Mary Ellen was determined to root out any potential male chauvinism on my part. If there is a little piglet in me, I have honestly tried to overcome it. It kills me to say this, but a strong marriage is based on equality. That's why I let her rake leaves, grill ribs and do most of the driving.

For three decades I have also shared with my wife the chores of loading and unloading the dishwasher. I've hated every single second of this responsibility. I'd rather clean the toilet, poke a bees' nest with a broom handle, or clean out the gutters with a teaspoon.

Last week my wife informed me that I was now forever relieved of dishwasher duty. "Just scrape the dishes and stack them in the sink," she told me.

"But why?"

"You're terrible at loading and it seems to get

worse by the day," she said. "Ever wonder why when you unload dishes the next morning, everything you flung into the machine willy-nilly has miraculously lined up perfectly in the appropriate slots? Who do you think did that?"

"Well, it takes almost an hour to run a load of dishes and I hear a lot of odd noises, so I assumed a mechanical realignment was one of the wash cycles."

"You just toss the dishes in, any which way. What are you thinking?"

"Mary Ellen, I load the dishwasher like I load our Maytag. I don't put socks in one part of the washing machine, then my pants in another. Why would I do that with cups and saucers?"

Mary Ellen says I'm getting progressively worse at unloading, as well. I simply dump the entire utensil holder into the kitchen drawer. Clankety-clank: mission accomplished. My wife has this odd notion that you should sort the knives, spoons and forks into their own compartments. She wants them separated—even before we set the table. What kind of a waste of time is that? Mary Ellen also thinks the soup bowls, salad plates and cups should be placed in the cupboard into matching individual stacks. Where's the pizzazz in that architectural structure?

She also says I've been messing up the inside of our fridge. Here again everything has its proper place. Who knew? So that's why the mustard has been moving from the top shelf to the fridge door. Why heads of lettuce have often crept south, ending up in this thing Mary Ellen says is called the "vegetable bin." Why was I never informed of this accessory? Milk, I have learned, should always be on the top shelf. Jars of sauces and prepared foods have to go on the third shelf. That's gotta be wrong because when I was six, I'd swear the pickles were always staring me right in the face. Going eye to eye with Kosher dills goes back to the Old Testament.

So, I am no longer permitted to load or unload the dishwasher. And I must leave my pickles, mustard and cream cheese on the counter so my wife can put them in their proper resting place. I may even have a shot at never doing laundry again. But I am not going to get complacent about my lack of accomplishments. There are beds not to be made and rugs not to be vacuumed. I'm very proud of myself. I'm doing the worst I can.

Clean Sweep

I received something interesting in the mail. It wasn't an exotic postcard from Maui; it was a thank-you note for a recent purchase I had made.

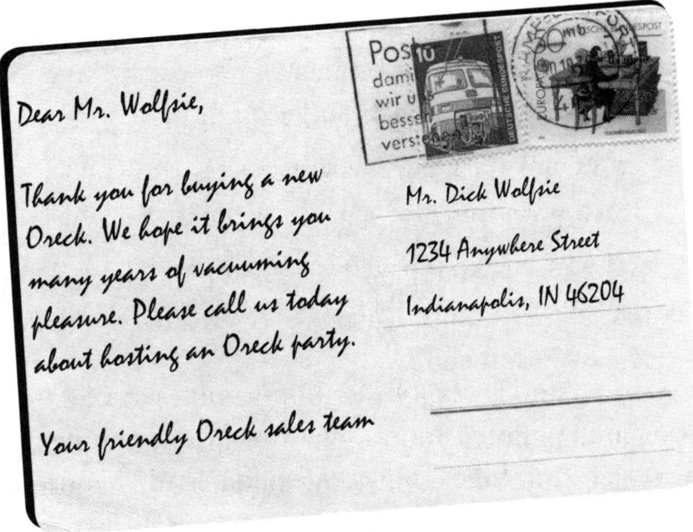

Dear Mr. Wolfsie,

Thank you for buying a new Oreck. We hope it brings you many years of vacuuming pleasure. Please call us today about hosting an Oreck party.

Your friendly Oreck sales team

Mr. Dick Wolfsie
1234 Anywhere Street
Indianapolis, IN 46204

The truth is that I don't have any intentions of spending a single enjoyable moment with my vacuum. I was a bachelor until I was 33 years old and I managed to maintain a very active social life without hovering over a Hoover or dallying with a Dirt Devil. In addition, I have always felt there is something frightening about vacuum cleaners. Every dog I have ever owned agrees.

It was a friendly gesture by Oreck, to be sure, although I have no recollection of a similar follow-up after the Wolfsies bought our nifty sump pump. And I've gone through all my previous correspondence and no one cared a whit whether I had a positive experience with our document shredder. As a general rule, I don't want annoying phone calls and letters asking me if I'm a satisfied customer. If I have a garbage disposal that is not disposing, the load of goop in my sink is a good indication that I'm not happy with my purchase. I'll take it from there.

When I had my car serviced, the dealership called me every other day for a week to see if I was happy with my new brake pads. I told them that I couldn't be more thrilled and that I'd be willing to throw a party for all their customers, so people could vent about some of the poor brake pad choices they've made in the past. (Assuming anybody is still around.)

Now, let's talk about that Oreck party. My wife and I are not big on "entertaining," the term my mother used for dinner parties when I was growing up. As a kid, I kept waiting for Mom to break into song when the guests arrived and for my father to commence a little soft shoe.

But what about a vacuum cleaner bash? I'm not usually at a loss for words, but I'd be stuck for snappy conversation while guests clustered around the artichoke dip. I took a speech class in college and once spoke off-the-cuff for 15 minutes on the topic "Life Before Rubber Bands." Nevertheless, the prospect of chatting with 20 people who shared similar cleaning devices was daunting.

"So, Dick, I understand that you and your wife have a new Oreck. Enlighten the group with some of your favorite moments."

"It's hard to pick our favorites. The night the bag of Fritos fell on the rug was unforgettable. We loved the time the dog shredded the down pillow. And Mary Ellen has a special place in her heart for Christmas morning when there were packing peanuts all over the living room floor."

I think Mary Ellen and I will pass on the Oreck party. We still have feelings for our first vacuum and it was tough saying good-bye. It wasn't easy for Kirby the past 25 years. He was the product of a bygone era. Until the day Kirby died, he pretty much remained in the closet.

A Dandy Story

"What are you doing?" asked my wife one Saturday morning.

"Nothing," I said, which is generally her first clue that I am up to no good.

"Nothing? You are peeking out the front door window. In fact, I've caught you doing this several times this past month. What are you looking at? Promise me you're not going to end up groveling in front of Judge Judy."

"Okay, Mary Ellen, I'll tell you what I am doing, but you are going to laugh. I'm waiting for dandelions to pop up."

My wife has observed a lot of my strange behaviors over the years, but it was clear that this latest admission rivaled my obsession last summer with the moles in our front lawn. What's wrong with an elaborate video taping system to better understand how these little hoodlums engage in their underground activity?

Let me explain the dandelion thing. I came up with a theory that there was no need to put down weed preventative on my lawn since everyone else in my neighborhood performs the pre-emergent ritual. I figured there was no chance for my lawn to be infected. I mean, where would the nasty seeds come from?

My theory, of course, was tragically flawed, though I am unclear why. By late April the yellow dandelion heads were poking up through the blades of grass, taunting me to respond to their infestation.

So now each morning I go out with my trusty weeder, carefully slide the device under the root system, then pop the pesky plant out of the ground. I am ashamed to admit this, but I really enjoy the process. Divesting an evil from my lawn, is liberating, especially when the plant has spread out in total defiance, only to be conquered by my trusty hand and eye. By the way, I refuse to spray Roundup on the offender. Did Arnold Schwarzenegger squirt the enemy?

But here's what's driving me crazy. On a typical morning, after I extract every single dandelion, I go into the house, read the paper, shower and have breakfast. Two hours later, there they are again, sunbathing on my front lawn.

Where did they come from? How did they get there? I can't get that kind of fertile response when I really need it. Three weeks ago, I reseeded a small area in my yard where the grass had died. A month later: nothing. Still as bare as a baby's . . . well, I think you get the picture.

I admire the dandelion's persistence and fortitude, so I am driven by a desire to see one pop up and bloom before my very eyes. Thus, I stare intently through the front door window hoping to see the actual blossoming of this ubiquitous weed.

But, alas, it is not to be. Maybe the dandelions know someone is watching. Perhaps nature's miracles would lose their magic if man could witness the growing process. My son, for example, went from 21 inches at birth to 70 inches in 18 years. I never saw him budge.

I still plan to keep an eye on my front lawn. Uh oh, it looks like I have to mow the grass again. Funny, I never saw that coming, either.

Down Under

My home office is downstairs. It was just a cellar when we moved into the house in the '90s, but we invested a little money to fix it up, so then it became a basement. I guess you could call it a finished basement. Apparently, it wasn't finished enough because the builder we hired said that for a few extra bucks he could add some additional touches and then we could call it our lower level. We didn't have that kind of money.

Our original plan was to make it a beautiful room where we could entertain guests, sip white wine and talk about good books and the current movie scene. Nowadays no humans are allowed downstairs except me and the men from Orkin.

We have a pool table that I bought in 1998 when I wanted to get my son interested in something other than video games. I thought if I kept going back to negotiate the best price, I might have a shot at meeting that Watson's girl.

We never have played pool. I use the cue sticks to wrangle cobwebs from the ceiling. I can store a dozen suitcases under the base and the top of the table is the perfect nesting area for a year's supply of Bush's baked beans. Each side pocket holds a flashlight. Corner pockets? Duct tape, scotch tape, masking tape and electrical tape. And my wife said we'd never use the thing. Jeesh, what a pessimist.

Somewhere under boxes of old paperback books and smelly blankets is a futon, which we bought because we were told it was a cheap and convenient extra bed. It took three defensive linemen to negotiate the stairwell to get the thing down to the basement. I don't know what the mattress is made of, but the cat sees the unit as a condo—two beds and a bath, if you know what I mean.

I Googled 'futon' to find out the origin of the word. There were links to websites that discussed serious sleep disorders, including one called exploding head syndrome. I don't want to overreact, but I am keeping a close eye on that cat.

In 2000 I decided I wanted to learn to play the piano so I spent a hunk of money on this electronic gizmo called a Clavinova. It can be programmed to play 30 different instruments, create background rhythms, and magically produce chords. I don't have to do much of anything but sit there and make the next payment. I've put the Clavinova on eBay three times and have had about as much success as Sarah Palin did selling her Boeing 707.

We built a bar in the corner so guests could mosey over and have a nice cold one. But we never put in the fridge as we had planned. You can still mosey on over and see our new sump pump. Better hurry. We may actually install it any year now.

There is a huge green slab of wood resting against a wall, half hidden behind stacks of clothing and picture frames. I asked my wife about it. "That's a ping-pong surface, Dick. It fits over the pool table. I guess we've never used that, either."

I told Mary Ellen it was about time we invited some friends over and finally played some table tennis in our cellar. But first, I have a whole lot of beans to eat.

Lost in Space

The party's over. Our 30 guests have gone home, but I'm a little concerned. I can't find the cat's scratching post, the cordless phone that was on the living room table or my brand new bicycle helmet. Oh, and where's the dog's water bowl?

I'm not accusing anyone of anything. The truth is, all those things are somewhere in the house. I just haven't figured out where. Yet. You see, I put them all out of sight—and apparently out of mind.

My mother (and yours, I am sure) called it "straightening." Mom was always telling me to straighten my room. Straightening was simply rearranging the clutter, with no suggestion that anything was to be discarded. When you're a kid, you learn that hiding stuff is the fastest way to straighten.

To this day I am a compulsive straightener. So is my wife. I think we are the straightest couple in the neighborhood. I was in the Logans' house across the street once. They are not as straight. Not that there's anything wrong with that.

With our party a few hours from starting, it was time to straighten extra well. That's when the old toaster, the dog's bowl and the iPod were squirreled off into some corner, rolled under a bed or crammed in the back of a closet. The good news is that our home has never looked so neat. The bad news is that I really like toast, enjoy music, and now the dog **may have to** drink out of the toilet.

The downstairs bathroom was sufficiently in order, but with more than two dozen people at our bash, it was possible that my "office" upstairs might attract some additional traffic. "Hide everything," said Mary Ellen. "Your bathroom is a disgrace."

That's when I grabbed all my medications off the counter, my electric toothbrush, the Norelco shaver, a gallon-size bottle of Scope and three hairbrushes and hid them in the . . . well, I put them under the . . . I lodged them behind the . . . I have no clue where they are.

The same thing happened in the dining room. Because we seldom use that area, the dinner table had become the depository for bills and assorted unimportant important papers. My wife has always been concerned about leaving material like this out in plain sight. She thinks it all should be secured in a place where no one can find it. The party was last week and I still can't locate my calculator, the Chase bank statements, or my life insurance policies. Mission accomplished.

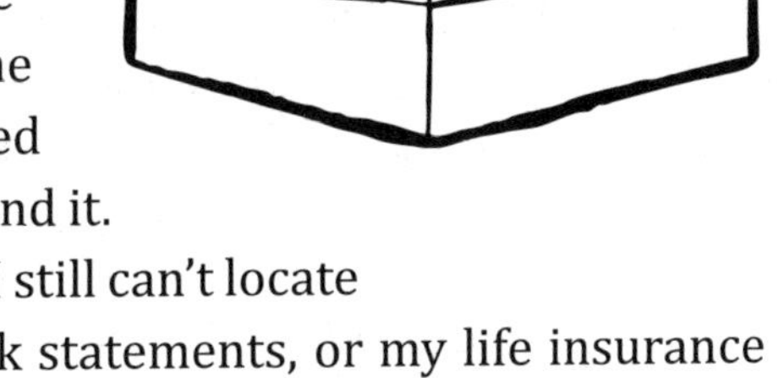

I spent most of the past week looking for things and I've had some success. I located a portable DVD player I had crammed in the back of the broom closet, an old dehumidifier that I had wedged under the ping-pong table, and a huge box of assorted electrical wires and transformers that I had stuffed behind the recliner in the living room. That was from our Super Bowl party—the year the Colts won.

The morning after this party, I couldn't brush my teeth, comb my hair or take my Lipitor. Fortunately, when I finally got in the shower, I found it all piled up in the tub. Eventually everything will show up. But we really miss the dog.

Washed Up

We were both afraid to go into the room. We walked back and forth in front of the door for several days, avoiding the inevitable. Things were piling up outside and I knew that we couldn't hold out indefinitely. But I didn't want to be first; nor did Mary Ellen.

Our son Brett was home from college for winter break. "Brett, you try it. I'm just not comfortable with the whole idea," I said. "It's so big. And so blue. I'm scared to death of it."

"Dad, they're just laundry machines."

Easy for him to say. He's young. He grew up in a high-tech world of computers, iPods, and Internet surfing. When I was his age, Post-it notes were the rage. Now, I was faced with technology I would have to master sooner or later. Our old washer-dryer set had been on the fritz and as luck would have it, my wife won a brand new set of appliances in a raffle.

They arrived last week and I watched as the two behemoths were installed by a crack technician. "Don't I get instructions?" I asked, expecting a short tutorial. Instead, I was handed a 74-page manual. In four languages.

I stared at the two appliances for several minutes. Our laundry room looked like the cockpit of a 747. Between the two machines there were over three dozen buttons. Each not only lit up when touched but emitted a series of short annoying beeps as if it were trying to communicate with me like in the movie *Close Encounters of the Third Kind.*

Our old washer had two settings. Going from a normal cycle to a gentle cycle is not something a man does lightly, so I never messed with that. My wife sometimes ventured there, but for the most part, the Wolfsies put a normal spin on things.

I don't have a lot of confidence with washers, in general. My wife won't let me load the dishwasher because she says I don't respect the slots. I think this is a design flaw inherent in the product. When I load my camera I have very few decisions to make. I don't have a gun, but seems to me that the people who manufacture firearms have made it pretty clear where to stick the bullet, so that even after a few Coors Lights you'll get it right.

Somehow I end up melting all the Tupperware. I'm okay with cups and glasses, although my wife claims it matters which end is up, which I think is just an affectation on her part. Mary Ellen also has this thing about rinsing the dishes *before* I put them in the washer, but you don't run underwear under hot water before throwing them in the clothes washer. I'm right, aren't I? I can see you nodding your head.

I scanned the buttons on the new Whirlpool and eyed the dial that gave me options such as silk, quick wash or wool. One setting said hand washables, but I wasn't going to stick my mitts in there while that monster was turning. The setting for big, bulky items was okay with me, but I think the whole idea of it scared the dog half to death. One setting said sanitize, which I had thought they threw in with every cycle.

The dryer had a setting called super hot, which I told my wife was especially for her. If we had been in a fancy restaurant that might have gone over well, but we were standing in a room knee-deep in dirty sheets and pillow cases.

My favorite button is the one that adjusts the volume of the other buttons so that if you are down in the basement, you can hear the machine upstairs alert you that you are no longer washing, you are now spinning. I'm amazed Mary Ellen and I ever managed without this feature.

I have to go now. My socks are calling.

The Mouse that Roared

There is a mouse living in the Wolfsie kitchen. At least one. The dog knows it; the cat knows it. And my wife knows it. We're just trying to hide it from the neighbors.

We've had critter problems before, but there's a big difference between having mice in your kitchen and having, let's say, a woodchuck in your backyard. Having a woodchuck is something you can mention at a cocktail party and someday those same people will flock to your backyard for a cube steak cookout or sit in your kitchen and gorge themselves on your homemade guacamole. The fact that you have woodchucks does not diminish your stature in the community one bit or call into question your worthiness or cleanliness as a neighbor. This is not true of mice.

In fact, when news gets out you have woodchucks, people will call to chat about it. Some will suggest you tolerate the chucking. I mean, how much wood . . . never mind. A few folks may come over with beer to observe the woodchucks at work. What you thought was a real problem will instead make you the talk of the neighborhood.

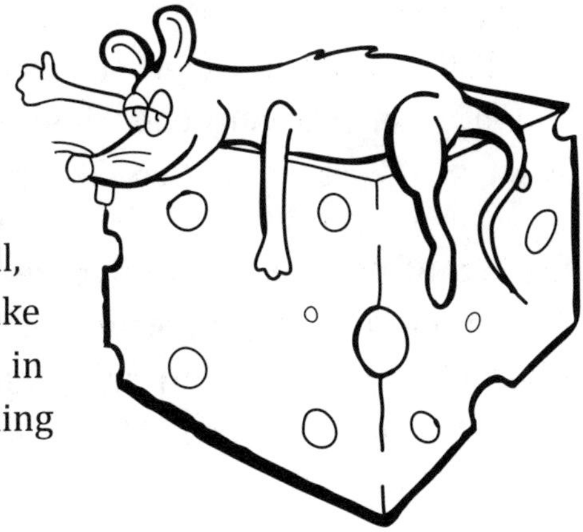

"Say, did you hear that Dick Wolfsie has woodchucks?"

"No, is that right? Well, leave it to an East-Coaster like Dick, a man with a career in broadcasting, to do something big and dramatic."

This is not the same reaction you get when word leaks out you have mice.

"Have you heard that Dick Wolfsie has mice?"

"You're surprised? He's from New York. And he's in television. Who knows what else is going on under his sink?"

Before I go any further, let me be honest and tell you that I'm not sure we have mice. I am sure we have one mouse, but despite my wife's insistence that we are infested with the creatures, I believe it is the same mouse every time. Debating this point has become almost surreal.

"Dick, I think it's several different mice. The first one acts nervous and shy. The other one is aggressive and dominant. And there's this one under the kitchen sink that seems lost."

"Mary Ellen, please don't do this. If you assign rodents a personality, it will make it that much more difficult to get rid of them."

"What do you mean by 'get rid of them'? Look, Dick, I want you to get rid of the mice, but I don't want you to ever tell me you got rid of them. I do not want any information about this. I hope this is clear."

"You don't want any specifics on how they died?"

"Do NOT mention the word 'die' in this house. Go Google 'mouse' and see if there's some catch and release program you can sign up for. Maybe there is a mice relocation project. I do not want to hear about how any mouse succumbed to some sick, barbaric trap you bought at Home Depot. And you be nice to Seymour, especially."

"Mary Ellen, please don't give them names. This is making it worse when I have to . . . well, you know . . . "

"Too much information! Too much information!"

So I took care of things. We no longer have any mice in our kitchen and I am pleased to say that Mary Ellen chooses to see me as benevolent and kind. She's convinced—and rightfully so—that I was humane and civilized in my task.

But the cat hasn't spoken to me in a week.

Naked Truth

I'm going to tell you a little secret and I hope you will keep it between us. If my neighbors find out, I might lose my position as Neighborhood Watch Commander, a post I sought and would like to retain for my remaining years in our cul-de-sac.

Okay, here goes: In the mornings, real early, I run out in nothing but my sleeping shorts to grab the morning paper. I say sleeping shorts, but let's call them what they are: underwear. They do come in some lovely designer colors and patterns and I think I could make a good argument in court that they are no more revealing than a bathing suit or a pair of Bermudas. Plus, I am inclined to continue this behavior because I have never seen a similar case on *Law and Order*.

I carefully time my 40-second dash every morning based on when our neighbors—Norm, Mark and Jeff—leave for work. I also know when their wives head for the office or drop the kids off at school. By the way, I time this so they do NOT see me. I don't want you to think I'm a total weirdo.

I perform this ritual 12 months a year—yes, even in the dead of winter. The only difference is that when the driveway is covered with snow, I tend to make a Three Stooges woo-woo-woo sound as I scoot back into the house on my tiptoes.

When you are my age, there are not a lot of exhilarating things to look forward to. Oh, I know that many people in their fifties and sixties are into skydiving, motorcycling and parasailing, but there's a limit to how many X-treme sports shows I can watch on cable. Plus, I'm too lazy to put my pants on.

My wife looked out the bedroom window Sunday morning, a day when it takes a little longer for me to scoop up the entire paper; then I had to venture out onto the front lawn to retrieve the K-Mart and Lowe's inserts that had blown away. Needless to say, I got a firm lecture from Mary Ellen.

"You are never, ever to go out on the driveway again in your underwear."

"Sleeping shorts."

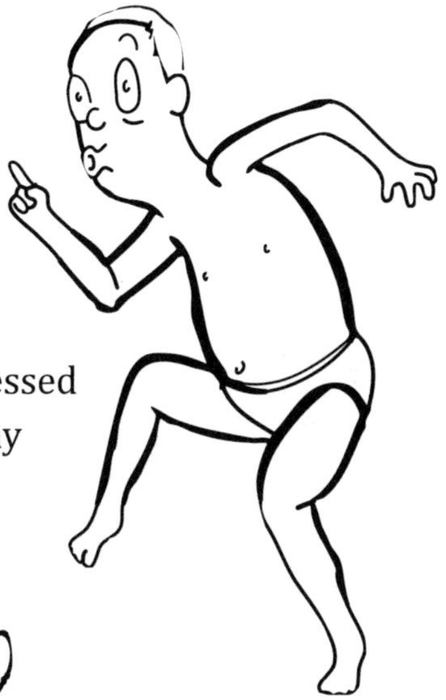

"Okay sleeping shorts. You are never to go out to get the paper in your sleeping shorts again. Ever. Is that clear?"

"But I don't want to have to get dressed to get the paper. It takes me out of my relaxed mode. What's the difference if I'm caught in my under . . . I mean my sleeping shorts? And anyway, I have it all timed perfectly. No one has ever seen me."

"Oh, fine, then why wear anything at all? Oh dear, did I really say that? Look, Dick, the discussion is over. Hey, why not teach the dog to get the paper?"

"Teach the dog to get the paper? After four years we're still working on the 'gimme your paw' thing."

I must admit, Mary Ellen did have a good idea. So this past week I've been quite successful in teaching Toby to fetch the newspaper.

But he sure looks silly in my sleeping shorts.

Not Even Remotely Funny

Good news out there for people like you and me who can never find their TV remote. I know this is a source of frustration, but I have always looked on the bright side. If I did not have to tear apart my couch at least twice a month and dive into the dark side beneath those cushions, I wouldn't have $235.89 worth of change in a cookie jar and I'd still be wondering what happened to my wedding ring and all our ballpoint pens.

No one can argue that a remote control is third only to movable type and the ShamWow for the world's greatest inventions. I became so paranoid about losing the remote that for a long time I wrapped a long piece of dental floss around it and then tied the line to the leg of the coffee table. I never lost the remote. And I remembered to floss 45 percent more often.

I have never understood why there are functions on the remote that are not on the TV console itself. Maybe I'm a little dense, but with all those buttons they jammed onto something the size of a stapler, why couldn't they put them on the set, as well? When I lose the remote, I spend 20 minutes on my knees in front of my flat screen with a tiny flashlight, hoping I can either change channels or turn the whole thing off without having to go down in the basement to trip a circuit breaker. I expressed frustration about this to my wife, claiming there was no other apparatus in the world where you can't control the device from the unit itself.

"What about those remote controlled airplanes?" she asked.

Mark Twain was right. There's nothing more annoying than a good example.

One company may have solved the disappearing remote problem. They will soon introduce a new TV set that obeys commands based on hand and body movement. This technology is called gesture recognition. (It's a concept we are all familiar with when we cut someone off on 465.) "The TV has a camera and will recognize you if you are in front of it," says the manufacturer. This intrigued me because I've been in front of a camera for 30 years, and I'm still having a heck of a time being recognized.

The premise is that you can wiggle your fingers, point up or down or make various other motions and the TV will respond. I always make one particular gesture when I watch a certain cable news show, so I'm concerned that the technology may get confused and take me to channel one by mistake.

Let's say my wife and I have retired for the evening. She watches as I flex my fingers and rotate my palms. "Ooh, are you going to give me a massage?"

"No, I'm trying to turn on David Letterman."

Advances will not stop with the TV remote. One day I'll observe Mary Ellen waving her hands in front of the stove. "Dick, I'm turning the skillet up to high. Please, don't make any false moves. I don't want to start the espresso machine."

Truth is, I have no interest in food preparation. I don't know how to use our Cuisinart or our convection oven. So, this state-of-the-art technology won't change my life a bit. When I walk into the kitchen, I still won't lift a finger.

Time in a Bottle

We hadn't cleaned our kitchen pantry in years. The fridge gets a good once-over every month when we wipe off the shelves and throw out any food item that has developed a green slime. I've had to toss out a lot of good guacamole dip based on this criterion.

As my wife started yanking stuff out of the pantry, I heard her gasp as she examined each of the jars and cans. Apparently, we had a lot of old purchases that had squirreled themselves away in the back. I'm not a big fan of discarding perfectly good food, but I do recognize, for example, that if you go to make a sandwich and there is a layer of blue-green fuzz over the top of the whole wheat bread, you only have a two-day window of opportunity to consume it before it could go bad.

In the back of the closet, we found Greenie Hard Chews for dogs. They would have been for our first dog back in 1981. The box said they were "best used" by August of '86. *What could go wrong with them?* I wondered. Would they turn greener, get harder, even chewier? That worked for me, and probably for the dog. Back in the closet they went.

Then my wife handed me a bottle of Bookbinder Cocktail Sauce for shrimp. It said: "Use by October 1997." It looked fine, although I think shrimp sauce is supposed to be bright red, not black with maroon specks. I opened it and gave it a sniff. It smelled better than the fresh shrimp that had been in our fridge for only 36 hours. But I chucked it.

We found some Orville Redenbacher Popcorn and under Orville's picture it said "Expires May 1995." I put the jar back because I think that might have referred to Orville and not the popcorn.

We found some protein cereal bars that have the same shelf life as the cardboard box they come in. I'm not sure they are still going to be tasty, but I put a few in my glove compartment in case I ever get locked in my car and need a small crowbar.

There was a jar of honey, but I couldn't read the expiration date. I tried to pry the cap off, but it wouldn't budge. I ran it under hot water and banged the lid on the side of the counter. Maybe the top said: "Can't be opened after August of '01."

There was also jar of tartar sauce that had no expiration date at all, but it did say "Famous since 1877." I'm thinking this may have been a 100th year anniversary edition of the product, so I got rid of it. Anything that backwards spells rat rat, you need to be careful with.

Finally, we found a bottle of Hidden Valley Ranch salad dressing. I think the name tells it all. It had hidden from us for 17 years.

In an effort to economize and be less wasteful, the Wolfsies decided to prepare a dinner out of food that probably should have been discarded.

Popeye Spinach (Best if used by December of '07)
Artichoke Hearts (Enjoy by March '06)
Tomato Soup (Purchase by April '07)
StarKist Tuna (Put in toxic landfill after October 2002)

We wanted something to accompany the dinner, and sure enough, we found a bottle of wine in the closet. I poured it down the drain. You can take a chance with a can of asparagus from 2001, but a bottle of Merlot from 1986 was asking for trouble.

Trouble Brewing

I don't remember the last time I cleaned out the fridge in our garage. I've been heaving leftovers in the old appliance for a decade, like it was some kind of trash compactor. I don't believe in wasting food, so it was killing me yesterday to throw away perfectly good six-year-old tomatoes and what must have once been a very crisp cucumber.

It was when I removed one of the vegetable bins for a quick hosing that I first set my eyes on it. Now I know the excitement Richard Leakey must have felt when he gazed upon the skeletal remains of our early human ancestors. There, wedged behind condiments on the bottom shelf was an unopened bottle of The three brothers were grinning at me, chilling out after 10 years on ice in the back of my Kelvinator. Yes, gentlemen, there is a Three Stooges Beer. Unfortunately, they have stopped production. No Curly Light or Moe Extra Dry, either. Sorry!

The bottle was part of an assortment of exotic brews, a thank you from Gleaners Food Bank for emceeing one of their fundraising events. At the time, I wrote about the gift in my newspaper column, reflecting on how Three Stooges Beer would have made four years of college majoring in early American literature much more bearable. Why would I curl up in my frat house with a can of Budweiser when I could get wasted with the world's funniest threesome?

So, men, what happened to Three Stooges Beer? Forgive me, but I blame the ladies. Stranded in the Sahara Desert, mouth parched, near death—no woman would drink a Three Stooges Beer. You knew this, of course. We all instinctively know that women hate anything that has to do with the Three Stooges. If they won't laugh at them, they certainly won't chug them. You might as well offer them a Jerry Lewis Chablis. In fact, that's why most of you men have never heard of Three Stooges Beer. For years, a dedicated band of women were buying this product and dumping it at chemical waste sites.

When women shop for food, they prefer made-up brand names likes Mrs. Paul and Sara Lee. Honestly, did your Aunt Millie ever make you laugh? The guys prefer real military men like Colonel Sanders and Captain Morgan. I like the name Einstein Bagels. I can see Albert in my mind's eye, shuffling downstairs in his robe for one with a shmear of cream cheese. I even have a slogan: Einstein Bagels: Not just a recipe, a formula.

More food should be named specifically after comedians. Sadly, I don't think Madison Avenue would take the chance of alienating women shoppers. I asked my wife if she'd ever buy Abbott and Costello Mayonnaise . . .

"Would there be Hellmann's on the shelf?"

"No, Mary Ellen, assume this is the only brand available."

"Well, in that case, I still wouldn't buy it. I would buy Brad Pitt Olives. Do they make Mel Gibson Mustard?"

I'd buy Laurel and Hardy fish sticks. There's room in my fridge for Stephen Colbert Cottage Cheese and a place in my pantry for Rodney Dangerfield Tomato Soup. Jeff Foxworthy Tuna would make a dandy sandwich. And for you senior citizens, wouldn't a container of Betty White Yogurt really hit the spot right now?

I know what you are wondering: "Dick, will you open the bottle and drink the beer?" I might. And then I'll regret it and smack myself in the head.

MOPEY ABOUT MEDIA AND MECHANICS

Letters from Dick Wolfsie

My good friend Patty Spitler is the host of *Pet Pals* on a local TV station every Saturday morning. She asked me to join the show's fan website where I could view photos of dogs and cats and post digital shots of my own furry friends.

I logged into the *Pet Pals* sign-up page and after entering some preliminary data came face to face with a CAPTCHA. This is not a breed of dog like a Shar Pei, but both are equally shmushed together.

A CAPTCHA is the security feature that requires you to re-type a series of hard-to-read letters and numbers exactly as they appear on the screen before being issued a password or given permission to access a website. It ensures a real human being is taking advantage of the various promotional opportunities.

Without CAPTCHA, renegade software programs could amass a boatload of $10-off coupons to Bucca de Beppo, creating a scarcity of giant spicy meatballs right here in Indiana.

Apparently computer software programs can defeat a grand master in chess and beat the pants off the reigning Jeopardy champions, but they can't read really bad handwriting. Deciphering chicken scratch was never a problem for my elementary school teachers, but if my printing was as bad as CAPTCHA's when I was back in the fifth grade, I'd still be back in the fifth grade.

On the *Pet Pals* site I carefully hunted and pecked the curious series of letters into the box. Let's see: was that two V's in a row or was it a W? Was that KLo or Kb? I had no idea, so I took a wild guess. INCORRECT, the prompt berated me. Graciously, they offered me another chance.

I took out my reading glasses and peered onto the screen. I typed with only one finger to increase my accuracy. There were two words this time with a squiggly line through them. Some letters looked like caps and others didn't, but some you couldn't tell because they were back-to back with another figure. Some of the numbers appeared as if they were doing the tango together. Why was this so difficult? I just wanted Patty's fans to see Toby with his adorable St Patrick's Day hat on. I wasn't trying to join the CIA. I made another attempt.

INCORRECT repeated the prompt. Or was it InCorRecT?

I became so frustrated that I tried the audio CAPTCHA, intended for folks with vision issues, which clearly included me. In this version of CAPTCHA you hear a cacophony of indistinguishable sounds, much like in a crowded restaurant, then suddenly a recognizable word emerges like ORANGE, then more murmuring, then another, maybe BATHTUB, just as an example.

I enunciated each word I heard into my computer's microphone, not aware my wife was listening at the foot of the stairs:

RETREAT . . . ALAMO . . . VIOLIN . . . CHRYSANTHEMUMS . . . SWITCHBLADE

Mary Ellen was frightened by my incoherent rant. She inched back up the steps without making a sound.

I finally got into the *Pet Pals* website and I also managed to convince my wife I had not totally lost my mind. How did I do that? Do I have to spell everything out for you?

Cell Mate

It's not easy being Dick Wolfsie's cell phone. He's misplaced me 72 times in the past 18 months. Of course, I was never really lost. I knew exactly where I was, but have you ever tried to get this guy's attention?

I'm also all chewed up because his destructive dog likes to gnaw on my corners. I've become a cellular cookie, a mobile meatloaf, if you will. It's not a job I'd call home about. Next time, no pets.

Here's my story: On Sunday, I'm at the Shrine Circus at the Fairgrounds where Dick is doing a TV show. I'm in his pocket. No, now I'm resting on top of a clown cannon. Oops! He shoves me under his coat on a chair. I'm lost. He starts looking all over for me. Now he's borrowing a phone. He's going to call me. Uh oh, my battery is running low. I ring. Success!

We're headed home. He throws me in his briefcase and I land in a tiny hidden pocket next to a health insurance card that has been missing for the last month. He'll never find me here. I can peek out the tattered corner of the leather bag and see him.

Monday: I'm still in this briefcase, but he doesn't know I am missing because he hasn't left the house all day and most calls go to his regular phone. It's really dark in here.

Tuesday: He's looking for me. He's checking every coat pocket . . . Wait! Here he comes toward his briefcase. He peers into the abyss, but he can't see me. Call me! Call me before it's too late! He heads for his desk phone. I go right to voicemail. My battery is dead.

Wednesday: He heads back to the Fairgrounds to see if he left the phone there. I'm right next to him in his briefcase. Oh, the irony. No, they didn't find a cell phone at the Circus. Back home, he searches the entire car, including where I once slid under one of the floor mats. The rest of the day he looks everywhere, including in his briefcase four more times. Boy could I use a charge.

Thursday: He's given up. We head to the cell phone store. Time to buy a replacement. His contract is almost expired so they make him a deal on a sexy new model with a lot of features so he can get email he'll never learn how to access, and take countless accidental pictures of his ear. He falls for it. Men! The salesperson destroys me digitally on the computer. I am cellular non grata.

Dick gets back in the car and we head home. Once in the house, he starts reading the new instruction booklet. He's confused and frustrated. He has underestimated the power of familiarity. He's starts pushing buttons wildly. He hasn't had this look on his face since he bought a new toaster.

Suddenly, a flash of insight. He stares at his briefcase. He walks over and turns it completely upside down and shakes it.

Out I fall. Also his insurance card. And a set of keys from his last car and his sister's Happy 55th Birthday card. (She's 57 now.)

He embraces me and kisses my mangled corners.

Friday: We head back to the phone store. He tells the clerk he doesn't want his new phone, that he'll eat the cost. He wants his old friend back. My circuits well up.

"Okay," says the perplexed customer service rep, "but keep the new phone, in case you lose the old one again."

"Yeah," says Dick, "like that would ever happen."

Facing My Habits

I have mixed feelings about reconnecting with my high school friends on Facebook. I look at their photos and wonder why they all got better grades than me back in the 60s, but they're not smart enough to post a 25 year-old photo so they don't look little old men and women. As Mr. Grossman used to say in Geometry, "Do the math." The expression became quite popular.

The other day, I did update my photo. There was quite a stir in cyberspace. It motivated some old acquaintances to reminisce about the old days.

First there was Bernie's message, which included the following observation:

> *Dick,*
>
> *You know how you used to bounce your leg in class and how it drove the teachers crazy? Well, I picked up that habit from sitting next to you for three years. I still do it. Thanks a lot. By the way, do you still lose stuff all the time?*

Then there was a note from Ethan:

> *Dick,*
>
> *Remember in high school when you reported your car stolen from the student parking lot but later realized your mother had driven you to school that day? Are you still a space cadet?*

Finally, from Charlene:

> *You were always so adorable. I must have been crazy to have dumped you after the prom. Do you still whistle? Like how annoying was that on a date? I'm assuming you also stopped shaking your leg. Are you still scatterbrained?*

Do I still do all those things? I know I hadn't stayed on top of my geometry, European history or chemistry, but had I also neglected my habits? I knew my wife would be objective.

"Yes, you whistle," said Mary Ellen. "You've done it our entire marriage. You do it when we're in the car and when you're in your office downstairs. You also whistle in the morning. Do you know how abnormal that is?"

"Why?"

"Why? Because 99 percent of all the men in the world hate their jobs. Name one other person who whistles on the way to work.

"I can name a few: Dopey, Grumpy, Sleepy . . . Okay, how about that leg thing? Does it annoy you?"

"You bounce your leg when you watch TV, when you eat meals and when you read the paper. Sometimes I want to go into the garage, get some duct tape, wrap 1,000 feet of it over your right leg and secure it to the chair."

"Okay, but my question was: Does it annoy you? And do you think I'm spacey?

"Let's see, in the last month, you found your cell phone in the freezer, you found your car keys in the dog food bowl and last night you found your appointment book in the broom closet.

"Remember, Mary Ellen, there *was* a time I couldn't find anything."

I was depressed, but I think Charlene's note hurt the most. I emailed and told her that after all these years I still had wonderful remembrances of prom night. I also told her I had matured and was no longer spacey. I received this response the next day.

> *Dear Dick,*
>
> *Thanks for the email. I'm so happy you have fond memories of the prom. Are you sure you're not spacey, anymore?*
>
> *Sincerely, Ethan.*

Facing My Problems

Are you addicted to Facebook? Do you want to dump your Facebook page and get an actual life, and you need help finding all the places you have to click to make your profile disappear? It's called the 1,200-Steps Program. You'll be completely anonymous. Doesn't that sound attractive for a change?

Right now 45 total strangers are waiting to see if I am going to friend them or quietly ignore them. The Hyatt Hotel in downtown Indy asked to be my friend. Their request began: "Hi, Dick." I think it's weird when a building calls you by your first name.

Then I noticed stuff had appeared in my profile that I did not put there. In the "I Like" section it said that I was fond of Latex Novelties. Fortunately, my son explained to me that it was the name of a rock group. I'm equally perplexed as to how that got on my page.

The idea behind all this networking is knowing people who know other people. For example: I know that Charlene Reynolds and I have 12 mutual friends. The problem is that I don't know Charlene Reynolds.

If people approached you this way before computers, you'd think they were crazy. "Hey, Jack? How are you?"

"Hi, Dick. This is your lucky day. I have a list here of 50 people you don't know from Adam. Why not give them a call? You could spice up the conversation by mentioning your latex obsession."

Occasionally, a personal survey pops up on my page.

"Do you think Dick wears a hairpiece?"

"Do you have any interest in seeing Dick without any . . . "

"Who would Dick save first if his kayak turned over, his dog or his wife?"

Look, I'm embarrassed repeating this stuff. Plus, I wasn't happy with the results, although my beagle was thrilled with my last answer.

I couldn't get those questions off my page. Whenever I ask someone for help editing Facebook stuff, I always get the same answer: "I don't know how to do that; you have to mess around with the settings." That's not what a rocket scientist says when there's a problem in a lunar module.

And what's with all the suggestions on this site? Albert suggested you read this. Mary has suggested this site. If I wanted suggestive ideas, I'd be on craigslist, not Facebook.

Now let's talk about Lauren Rosenberg. On my profile page there's a bio of her and a nice little ad about her PR firm in Arizona. I didn't put her there. I don't want her there. I don't have the foggiest idea who she is. But she is obviously awfully good at PR. I tried for two hours this morning to remove her from my profile. I moved my cursor over every part of her photo until I started feeling a little creepy about the whole process.

I don't want my wife seeing this attractive young lady right in the middle of my homepage. Between that and Latex Novelties, there's just so much explaining I can do.

The bottom line here is I really need to remove myself from Facebook. I'm spending too much time with my friends and not nearly enough time with my friends. If you want to convince me to change my mind, I look forward to your input. Isn't that what friends are for?

Fond Memories

I hired a tutor to teach me about the intricacies of Facebook, blogging, and tweeting. The original plan was to take a class on all this, but I get very distracted in large groups and can't concentrate. This is what happens to me in a movie, which is why I'm still not sure why Colin Firth was in drag at the end of *Mamma Mia!*

Christine, my able instructor, spent a great deal of time with me. She discussed privacy settings and asked if I was okay just having friends, or whether I wanted to have communication with people who were friends of friends. I went for broke and opted for friends of friends of friends because before computers, that's the same method I used to select a doctor to do my first colonoscopy. Oh, and to find a wife.

At one point, Christine asked me to publish something on my Facebook wall, to give me an idea of how the process worked. For lack of anything prepared, I typed the following:

> Thanks to Facebook, I have located three old high school girlfriends. Two of them don't remember me.

Proudly, I hit the enter button and made my note visible to all 1,600 friends, few of whom I really know, but Christine assured me that this is the kind of juicy tidbit that people who surf the Internet are looking for to liven up a dreary day.

Of course, there was no truth to what I had written on my wall. Trolling for old squeezes online would be frowned upon by Mary Ellen. So would my downloading questionable content from websites that she believes would have a detrimental effect on our marriage: do-it-yourself home improvement projects.

Within minutes, my Facebook page was abuzz with commentary about my post from former classmates. "Post," by the way, is a new term I learned, and I'm trying to get the hang of using it. Christine will be so proud.

So here are some of the posts that were posted in response to my post:

> Dear Dick,
>
> I was an old girlfriend. Can you find out how the others managed to forget you? God knows I've been trying for 45 years.
>
> Charlene

> Hi, Dickie,
>
> Try not using your maiden name.
>
> Ginny

> Hello, Dick,
>
> I'm not 100% sure, but I think we went to the senior prom together. Does that make you feel better?
>
> Barbara

Wolfsie,

Your name rings a bell. Oh yeah, you used to copy my homework, steal my pen and call me chubby. Gee, thanks for reminding me.

Andrea

Dick,

We graduated in l965. We're lucky we even remember high school.

Carol

Hi, Dick,

I remember you very well, but we never went out. Maybe it's the dating part that makes you so forgettable.

Sara

I was a little embarrassed about all these responses suggesting I didn't make much of an impression on women, but I hadn't progressed far enough in my instruction to know how to delete them, so I called my Facebook coach. "Hi Christine, it's Dick Wolfsie."

"Who?"

High Tech Wreck

I recently read an article about how the iPad "will totally affect your life." I know it will change mine. The toughest part of the technological revolution for me has been coming up with plausible reasons why I'm not going to buy each new gadget.

When I was in college, I used a manual Underwood typewriter. When electric typewriters became the rage, I fought it tooth and fingernail. I asserted that there was a downside to typing faster than you can think. Computers are even speedier so I use that excuse to explain the drivel I write.

My battle with technology really began in the '70s when I refused to buy Post-it notes because I felt they were a lazy way to remember things. My concerns did not make for sparkling cocktail conversation with a first date, although I didn't have a lot of first dates. I kept forgetting to show up.

When I first heard about fax machines, I was also resistant. I finally went out and bought one in 1980, but I had nothing to fax. Thirty years later, I still don't have anything to fax. Have you ever met me? Do I look like a person who has documents that need to get someplace in 30 seconds?

I remember the first time I saw someone with a cell phone. I was playing golf back in the early '90s and a guy was calling his wife on the third tee. Then his boss called him on the 4th tee.

And on the next hole his dentist's office called him. Avoiding people was the very reason I was playing golf. I relented and bought a cell phone, of course, but I haven't learned how to fully use it. I have never taken a photo with my phone. And the only text I have ever gotten was from AT&T trying to get me to cough up the bucks for an iPhone.

The big cellular providers are missing some good opportunities to market to older people. How about a cell phone with a metal detector in it, so I can go to Indiana Dunes and poke around for nickels in the sand? Or a gentle alarm to wake me from my nap to let me know it's time to go to bed?

Now, let's talk about tweets. Every day I get emails from people who say they are following me on twitter. At first that struck me as creepy, but wait: I'm not on twitter. So how can I be followed? Fine, you might as well also follow me to the ballet, the international turkey-calling contest, or a clogging demonstration. Good luck.

Reluctantly, I joined Facebook, but I still can't figure out how this whole thing works. The other day a lady was ticked at something I wrote so she posted a note on my wall. Why are people writing on my wall? Were they brought up in a New York subway? Now the whole world knows what a jerk I am. This was supposed to be a secret.

Just to be cool, I bought a Kindle, one of those hand-held doodads that downloads entire books to view on an electronic screen. I do miss the feel of real paper, though. So I'm using Post-it notes to mark my favorite pages.

Letter Perfect

There should be a law. A law against having phone numbers that denote words instead of, well, numbers. Hello! It's a phone number, not a phone word. There is a national organization that is dedicated to educating people about a common, but potentially serious, illness. Their phone number spells the name of the disease.

That makes the number easy to remember, but impossible to dial on your cell phone when you are in the car and have to watch the road, balance your coffee, and try to figure out where the PQRS button is.

I misdialed 1-800 DIABETES—and got some poor guy in Tipton named Moe who said he was tired of people calling him with medical questions. He asked me to mention in my book that he is happy with his blood sugar, thank you very much.

While trying to dial this number, I almost ran into an 8733, which is "tree" in touch-pad language, in case you haven't mastered this concept yet. I got so mad I probably said a number I shouldn't say in mixed company: 3687. Before you go running to your phone to figure this out or call the publisher to complain that I said some dirty digits, I simply picked four numbers at random. They don't spell anything. I don't think. Oh dear, I better go back and re-check. I wouldn't want any four-number words in a this book.

Now suppose I wanted to pay extra to have a phone number that represents a personal reference like I AM DICK. It's not that simple. Apparently, those same numbers for I AM DICK could spell a lot of other words or letter combinations. So there is a good chance someone else has beaten me to the punch.

I needed help so I went to www.phonespell.org where you can see what words your phone number might spell . . . assuming you have nothing better to do.

That's where I discovered that 426-3425 (I AM DICK) has almost 10,000 additional letter combinations. Here are some they thought were unforgettable. GAN-E-IJC, BN-EH-AL or IC-MFG-BK. See how much simpler it is to remember seven letters than seven numbers?

Now that I have checked the website, I know I will never be able to get I AM DICK for my phone number because there are so many other people with common names like IC-MEGAL or ICOD-IK who have probably been waiting for that number to become available for many years. And if you are from the planet GAMDIA-5 you'd have snapped this number up eons ago to make it easier for fellow aliens to remember how to reach you.

If you enjoyed this column, don't forget it was written by 3425. But you and I don't have to be so formal. You can call me 3.

On the other hand, if you feel this is another example of how I can write the dumbest stuff and still get paid, I think it is fair to say: You've got my number.

Manual Labor

Andy Rooney once did a segment about how he throws out the instruction booklets when he buys new electronic gadgets, but I'm the opposite. I save every one. I have a box with hundreds of them. I have never read one, but at least I'm smart enough to keep them. Just in case.

I have manuals for gizmos and doodads and appliances, many of which are long gone. If you want to know how to replace that ball on your IBM Selectric, I'm your guy. How about setting the correct time on your Betamax recorder? Give me a call.

I started to browse through the pile of booklets and learned a great deal. I found out my microwave has a filter. And I'm supposed to clean it every few months. The service manual said that frequent cleaning of these filters would enhance the performance of the appliance. For 25 years I've been shoving Swanson's Chicken Pot Pies in the unit and hitting HIGH. And 1,485 times in a row, they've come out the perfect temperature to singe the roof of my mouth. You should not mess with success.

I discovered that almost everything I own has a filter. I have a filter in the clothes dryer and one on my lawn mower. I have one on the vacuum cleaner. Apparently there's one in my air conditioner. Next thing you know, I'll find out there's one in my car. I suspect all these filters are clamoring for a periodic change. I've neglected them.

"Honey, when's the last time we changed the filter on the weed wacker?"

If you're a husband and have never asked your wife this question, it's worth seeing the expression on her face. If you're a wife, you might want to drop this bombshell on your hubby at dinner when you're out with friends.

Most of the other information in these brochures is totally useless to me because it involves more interaction with the product than the on-off switch. I'm an impatient person, so I turn right to the last page, just to see how it all ends. This is where you find the Troubleshooting Guide for Einsteins like me who can't figure out why:

THE VCR WON'T RECORD
THE SAW WON'T CUT
THE DOG WON'T HUNT

If I were writing these guides, I'd inject a little humor:

GARAGE DOOR REMOTE

Problem: You've destroyed three luggage racks on your car.

Solution: When you drive in, wait until the door is completely up.

ELECTRIC PENCIL SHARPENER

Problem: You end up with just erasers.

Solution: Quit watching *Jersey Shore* while using the device.

SNOWBLOWER

Problem: Snow will not discharge from the unit.

Solution: Try again in the winter.

BEER MUG

Problem: Your shoes are getting cold and wet.

Solution: Glass is being held at wrong angle. Point open end toward ceiling.

LAWNMOWER

Problem: Grass is not getting cut consistently.

Solution: Find new husband.

PORTABLE ALARM CLOCK

Problem: Doesn't tell time.

Solution: You may have put the batteries in incorrectly. This reverse polarity will substantially alter the universe, making time run backwards. It will be your fault.

For fun I tried to read the Troubleshooting Guide for the microwave again—this time in Japanese and Spanish, but the bulb on my reading lamp suddenly burned out. I sure hope I can find that manual.

myPHONE

My wife and I were on the couch experimenting with different positions. Mary Ellen prefers vertical but horizontal is more comfortable for me. That's one of the many choices iPhone users have.

We felt like kids again with our new 3G devices, although we didn't know why we needed so many G's. After all, James Cagney once whacked a guy for two G's, so three G's sounded like overkill.

Lately, I'm feeling hipper than ever. I increased my presence on Facebook and snapped up an iPod. My Kindle allows you to download books you want to read. The problem is that it also downloads books you don't want to read. The "Buy" button is very sensitive. If you smile approvingly or nod your head while browsing the thousands of choices, you've bought a book. That's how I got stuck with *The Great Pantyhose Craft Book, Mensa for Dummies* and *Sex after Death*.

I now have about 400 friends on Facebook, more than I ever aspired to. I copied all the names into my phone so when someone posts something earth-shattering, like: "2 squirrels in my yard today. Dog went crazy. See photo," I can give them a quick call and chat about it. To facilitate this, I use my new phone application called VLINGO, which is a voice activation system. You say a person's name into your smart phone and the next thing you know, the two of you are chatting away. I decided to call my Facebook buddy, Roger Atkins.

ROGER ATKINS, I said, with perfect enunciation and monotone pitch.

After a few seconds, I heard, "Hello, this is Roger."

"Hi, this is Dick."

"Who?

"Dick Wolfsie. We friended each other on Facebook."

"My friends don't usually bother me at 6 a.m. Why are you calling?"

"I'm calling everybody. I want to tell you about my new app. When I say 'Roger Atkins,' my phone recognizes your name and calls you."

"And now I recognize your voice. So if you ever call me this early again, I'm going to disconnect your head from your neck, if you don't mind some land-line lingo.

Later in the day, I called my wife at the university where she works. CALL BUTLER, I said into the phone. "Hello, this is Butler. How can I help you?"

"Yes, Mary Ellen Wolfsie, please."

"Who? Does she work in the showroom?"

"Huh?"

"This is Butler Toyota, Sir. Do you want sales or service?"

I tried four more times to reach my wife, but I kept getting the dealership. I was offered a free oil change if I promised to quit pestering them. I guess re-calls annoy the folks at Toyota.

I decided to learn everything there was to know about my phone, but mastering this device was overwhelming so I decided to learn one new thing each day until I knew it all. For example, I discovered that if you hold your finger on one of the app icons, it will wobble and vibrate on the screen. Why? I don't have a clue. I'll figure that out tomorrow.

The Secret Word Is

I received an email from the college where I was teaching, informing me that everyone on the faculty had to change the passwords we used to enter the university website.

An independent consultant had determined that many of the terms we were using to log in were what they called "weak passwords." I've been accused of a lot of things: a weak chin, a weak stomach, being weak in the knees. But having weak passwords? The nerve!

I thought I used some pretty nifty ones in the past. For example, I once used LOIS for my ATM account. Lois was the first girl I ever had a crush on, back in 1956. I know this was a good password because even Lois didn't know she was my girlfriend.

I needed help, so I went to the university website to learn more. They had posted a few guidelines.

It shouldn't be a word in the dictionary
It shouldn't be personal data
It shouldn't be a pet's name
It shouldn't be a person's name

Then they said, BE SURE YOU CAN REMEMBER YOUR PASSWORD.

Huh?

They asked me to offer some new passwords. I tried to sneak a few old favorites by them. Then they had the gall to rate them every time I recommended a new option.

I tried to revive LOIS but it was rejected, not only because it was WEAK, but because someone else was using it. I always suspected there was another guy back in '57. Now I had the proof.

Then I tried my date of birth, just to see what would happen. A big red flag came up and the prompt flashed: VERY WEAK, claiming it was too easy to figure out by a would-be hacker. I think I look younger than my age, so this really annoyed me. Not only that, but no one has remembered my birthday in 25 years so I wasn't real concerned about that info getting out.

I tried putting in BOB, who's my best friend, but they hated that. I think the prompt said: YOU HAVE TO BE KIDDING.

No, I needed a strong password, so I put in HERCULES. It was rejected as WEAK. Then I tried SAMPSON. This time, VERY WEAK. I don't think the people over at Information Services have read their mythology. It did answer the 3000-year-old question of who was stronger.

At one point I was so frustrated that I couldn't come up with a simple acceptable password, I ran my fingers haphazardly across the keyboard.

VERY STRONG, said the prompt. PLEASE REMEMBER TO WRITE YOUR NEW PASSWORD DOWN. Write it down? I had no idea what I typed. Was it KKDFJHG or was it YQWOKW? My fingers may have done the walking, but they weren't talking. My secret was safe with them.

I finally found a password that was acceptable. No, I'm not telling you what it is. I will say it was deemed VERY STRONG. Then the website asked me a series of personal questions so I could retrieve it if my memory failed me.

The name of your first girlfriend.

Your best friend's name.

Your favorite character in mythology.

This was a joke, right? Those wild and crazy guys at Information Services.

On second thought, here is my new password: J&U*HY*&3JG%7. I do want you to have it—just in case I can't remember it.

MOPEY ABOUT MARRIAGE

Book Deals

I hate to charge friends for books I've written. When they compliment me on a new publication, I'm tempted to say, "Ah, forget it."

Here's how a good businessman would handle this: "Oh, hi, Dick. I heard you have a new book of humor columns. You wouldn't remember me, but about 12 years ago, I ran into you at the old RCA Dome and we had a nice chat at half time. What do you say to that?"

"I say, $16.95."

But see, that's not how I handle it. What's the opposite of cha-ching?

My wife looks at the issue like the MBA that she is. "People who hate you aren't interested in buying a book and you're uncomfortable charging your friends and the fans who suck up to you. That covers about everybody. This is not a good business model. You have to be strong."

I promised her I would try—and I did for about a week—but it was soon evident that I needed a way to wiggle out of this agreement with my wife. And I figured it out over lunch with my friend, Jim.

"I'd like to get one those new books, Dick. How much?"

"Gee, Jim. I hate to charge you; we've known each other for 25 years, but Mary Ellen has this crazy notion that we have to save money for retirement.

"No problem, I'll get out my checkbook."

"No, I can't do it. Wait, I have an idea. You buy the book and I'll buy you lunch. How's that?"

"I don't want to nitpick, but that Reuben I'm eyeing is only $8.95. The book is $16.95. You're not trying to scam me, are you?"

"Get something to go, as well. Maybe a nice Greek salad and a bowl of minestrone. Come on, work with me."

We carefully examined the menu for the right combinations. One humor book for a steak sandwich and a side of fries, plus a ham and cheese on rye to go and a generous tip for the waitress. That's $21.95 on the nose. Unfortunately, Jim has a big mouth and blabbered my dilemma to the whole world. Later that day, I got a phone call . . .

"Hey, Dick. It's Tony, your old buddy."

"Tony? Tony Garwin? I haven't talked to you in ages."

"Just seems that way, Dick. Look my wife's birthday is coming up and I think she'd love your book."

"So how is Ginny?"

"No, it's Coleen, now. Boy, it has been a long time. Here's my idea. How about if you come over to the house, clean out the garage, detail my car and paint the cellar door?"

"Huh? Why would I do that?"

"Well, Jim said you feel guilty about charging friends for your book, so I thought that would make you feel better about things."

"You want me to do all that stuff because I'm charging you for one book?"

"No, I need three books. Mom and Dad are big fans, too."

I spent most of last Saturday at Tony's house doing a variety of odd jobs. I swept the basement, fixed the toilet, and cleaned the mud room. Let me tell you something from personal experience: being a writer is hard work.

Degree in Marketing

I'm in a lot of trouble. I tried to sneak in the back door without my wife seeing me, but I got caught with you-know-what on my breath: salami.

Yes, I had been out carousing. At Kroger. I was returning home with a bagful of goodies. I usually shop while Mary Ellen is at work so I can take my stash and squirrel stuff away without her noticing what I bought. I have devised many clever places to hide questionable food choices, but none better than strapping the Meat Lovers Tombstone Pizza to the top of my SUV.

It's a terrible thing, this deception, but the tactic is required. Normally a sweet and understanding person, my wife is often critical of my supermarket purchases. She also questions my choice of books (she's not a fan of non-fiction), movies on DVD (no violence, please) and TV shows (she doesn't like people screaming at each other on cable news), but she generally keeps those opinions to herself and allows me to shuffle into my home office and indulge in private.

Back to my attempted covert entry into the house. Mary Ellen carefully eyed each item as I unloaded everything onto the counter . . .

EGGS: "Did you check the expiration date? Did you see three of them were cracked? These are not free-range eggs. And they're cheaper at Sam's Club. Brown eggs don't go with the new fridge."

FRENCH BREAD: "It's going to go bad. You never finish it. It gets hard as a rock overnight because you don't seal the package. After three days, the birds won't even eat it.

PISTACHIO NUTS: "Why did you buy those? You know we're just going to eat them. Almonds are better for you."

MILK: "A quart? It's so much cheaper by the gallon. And how many grown men still drink chocolate milk?"

HARD SALAMI: "That reminds me, did you remember to pick up your Lipitor at the pharmacy?"

Most of my purchases are based on a momentary hankering for a particular taste treat. Except for the occasional piece of dark chocolate, my wife doesn't really have food cravings like I do. If Mary Ellen turned to me one night and said, "I am dying for a grilled bratwurst with sauerkraut and a dill pickle," well, I can tell you right now, I'd want to check her photo ID before we spent the night together.

Last week I had this yearning for a jumbo shrimp cocktail. By the time I got to the store, I had lost that desire, and opted instead for a quart of Ben and Jerry's Chunky Monkey. This poor nutritional choice required finding the perfect hiding place at home to avoid my wife's disapproving eye. I can't use the space under the back porch. Even the dog has figured out that's my prime wintertime location for stockpiling frozen delights.

Another drawback to this trickery is that I forget where I've hidden things. Doritos in the laundry cabinet, Slim Jims in an old eyeglass case, and Peppermint Patties stacked up in the back of the medicine cabinet. Who can keep track of all this?

Truth is, I get a kick out of this game of Hide and Eat. I recently stuffed a Hostess Twinkie under my pillow. Before we drifted off to sleep, Mary Ellen made me promise to quit eating junk food. I told her I'd sleep on it.

Talking Heads

My wife and I were relaxing on our backyard deck and after swatting a few mosquitos, I said, "You know, Mary Ellen, we should look into screening in this area."

"Yes, Dick, you've been saying that every year for the past 15 years."

A few minutes later I mentioned how quickly the summer passes once July 4th weekend is over.

"I know, you say that every year around this time."

I also remarked that the neighbors don't grill out as often as we do. Apparently I had made this observation before. Several times.

Suddenly, I felt this great pressure on me. After thirty-one years, I apparently didn't have a single new thought to offer. I had always prided myself on my creativity, but clearly I was no longer very snappy with my repartee after three decades. Several moments of uneasy silence followed. Mary Ellen finally spoke . . .

"When it gets this hot, I think about cutting my hair shorter."

"Where have I heard that before?" I asked.

At that moment, we both realized we needed a way to jazz up our conversations. My wife had an idea . . .

"I read this article in the doctor's office, I think it was in *Cosmo*, that might be a solution

I've seen some of those covers *of Cosmopolitan* and I was just praying that was where she saw it. Just my luck, it was from *Good Housekeeping*. Mary Ellen said the writer recommended that long-time married couples should pretend they are having a first date. That would make for an exciting and potentially romantic evening.

It seemed like a silly idea at first, but I decided it was worth a try. On Friday night I asked Mary Ellen out for the next evening, which annoyed her because she said I was assuming she wouldn't be busy or maybe had plans to wash her hair. To be really suave, I went outside the house Saturday night and rang the doorbell, like it was a real date. I thought that would make a big impression on her, but she's no dummy and realized I had simply forgotten my keys. We drove off in the car.

"What shall we talk about tonight, Dick?"

"If this were a first date, we'd probably chat about movies we've each seen."

"Okay, great idea. I just saw Woody Allen's *Midnight in Paris*."

"I saw that, too."

"I know, Dick, we saw it together."

"Gone to any good restaurants lately, Mary Ellen?"

"No, my husband likes to go to the same places all the time."

"Mary Ellen, you are not supposed to have a husband. This is a first date. What kind of a jerk do you think I am, going out with a married woman? Let's try travel. Have you ever seen the Pyramids?"

"We went last year. How could you forget?"

"I didn't forget. I'm making conversation. That was the whole point of this."

"Well, it's getting too weird for me. I feel like I'm dating a man who's lost his memory.

We tried everything that people would chat about on a first date: music, religion, politics. Honestly, we didn't hit it off, but there must have been something brewing on some level because despite a dismal first date, we both ended up back at my place.

Weighty Decision

My wife casually mentioned to me the other night that I had a pathetic looking chest. While I suppose your better half is permitted to assess your upper half, I'd suggest not responding in kind. She thinks my body lacks definition, but I disagree. You can look it up in the dictionary under scrawny. Women are definitely more interested in men having muscles than a sense of humor. No female has never said: "I wish Matthew McConaughey would put his shirt back on and tell more jokes."

I used to go to a gym to play racquetball, and I'd see men and women fine-tuning their physiques, yet I wasn't inspired to fiddle with my own. Never really interested in the pure pursuit of brute strength, I would watch weightlifters during their routine. They'd pick up a heavy thing, then they'd put it down again. Such indecision.

After this stinging critique of my body, I read in *Prevention* magazine that when you reach 45 years of age, you begin losing one percent of your bone density and muscle mass every year. Old photos of me from high school show there was very little mass to start with, although some did roll in across my midsection in the early '80s. Density? I asked Mary Ellen about that, but she said not to worry, that I'm as dense as I've ever been—and she's not one to just toss out compliments.

I was embarrassed into starting a moderate body- building regimen. I don't go to the gym to work out, however. I do everything at home, in the reclining position, while watching cable news in the evening. Why didn't I think of this 15 years ago? I still wouldn't like Sean Hannity, but at least I'd be buff enough to throw king-size pillows at the TV from a prone position. Some of my other favorite moves are curls, extensions and squats. There are two techniques I don't perform: abductions and snatches. I don't need any more legal trouble after getting caught walking out of Dick's Sporting Goods with a set of free weights. Hey, that's what the sign said.

I'm making progress. Thursday I "bed-pressed" a hefty amount: 18,000 grams. It sounds impressive when counted the way the British do. I took one really heavy dumbbell and managed to hoist it over my head. When I put it down, the dog scooped it up in his mouth and buried it outside.

Mary Ellen, who regularly works out with a trainer, says my new resolution to lift things is a good sign. She's hoping it will carry over to lifting a finger around the house to help. Or picking up the check when her brother and sister-in-law come to visit. As for me, this has all helped lift my spirits. I can now hold a six-pack out in front of me, arms parallel to the ground, for an entire TV commercial.

A few days ago, one of my macho neighbors helped me lug a huge barbell up to the second floor of our house. My hope was that after a few months working out with some of the lighter weights, I would one day be able to lift this new behemoth all by myself. Mary Ellen thought it looked ugly in our bedroom. So she took it down to the basement.

Dog Tired

My wife was exasperated. "I can't handle this any longer," she said. "I'm all for love and commitment but enough is enough."

"I understand, Mary Ellen. I feel terrible."

"Dick, I know that snoring is not intentional. But it has some devastating effects on a marriage. What are you going to do about it?"

"I'll call the vet first thing in the morning."

Toby shot me a glance. He knew we were talking about him—dogs always sense that. Things had gotten out of hand the last few weeks. It wasn't his occasional snort that kept us awake; it was a full-blown, get out of my way, foghorn. He was also waking himself up every night, which made him cranky the next day. He really needs his 19 hours.

What led to the sudden onset of Toby's problem? His recent knee surgery had slowed him down a bit, resulting in a modest weight gain, which is a factor in snoring. I had observed no increase in smoking or alcohol consumption in the hound, another common cause.

True, I had promised Mary Ellen I would call the veterinarian, but first I did an advanced Google search to see if others were lying awake at night thinking about this problem. Apparently, there's a real epidemic of sleep disorders in the canine world: narcolepsy, jet lag, insomnia, night terrors and restless leg syndrome.

The first thing I learned was that dogs with short, flat faces—bulldogs, pugs, Pekingese—are more apt to snore. That makes it sound like bedding down with a horse is a better option for a good night's sleep.

One site suggested preventing your dog from dozing on his back with his paws up in the air, Toby's favorite slumbering posture in his doggie bed. When the snoring commences, roust the dog out of his deep sleep, then abruptly flip him over on his stomach. Mary Ellen thought this sounded like a good idea because that same method worked on me several years ago.

I'm no canine expert, but if Brutus the Rottweiler is keeping you up at night with his snoring, you might heed the time-honored maxim: "Let sleeping dogs lie . . . and snore."

In order to keep your dog on his tummy, one pet owner suggested gluing a tennis ball on a leather belt and wrapping it around the dog's torso, so the bulge on his back would prevent him from rolling over. I tried this with Toby but he was very adept at twisting himself into a knot, snatching the ball from the strap and then dropping it on my head so we could play fetch at two in the morning.

One woman recommended nasal strips, but sticking one of those on a beagle's nose is like trying to keep a bandage on a peeled banana. Another idea was giving your dog a nice foam rubber pillow to prop his head up at night, thus opening his nasal airway. Toby loved the pillow. Every bite of it.

My wife concluded that the only way to solve this problem was to sleep in separate rooms. She was right. The next night I got some great zzz's. I'm not sure about Mary Ellen and the dog.

Failure to Lunch

During 30 years of marriage my wife has made dinner for me 6,700 times. This is simply an estimate. I'm not some weirdo who keeps careful track of things like this, although it is interesting that I've cleared the table 6,692 times. Now, how many times has Mary Ellen made me lunch? Zero. Nada. Never. We do have our Thanksgiving meal around noon, but I refuse to call this Thanksgiving lunch because it makes it sound like we're already digging through the leftovers.

So last week Mary Ellen decided to take some vacation days and bring home a few files to work on. Because I have a home office, I was willing to assist her with some basic needs. She asked if she could borrow my computer in the afternoons.

"Not a problem, dear. Sharing is what marriage is all about."

"And the fax machine?"

"What's mine is yours."

"Oh, this will be so much fun. And we can finally have lunch together at home."

Suddenly, the blood drained out of my head. I started to perspire. A twitch developed in my right eye and I doubled over in pain. She was bound to know I was not happy with that suggestion.

How do you tell someone after 30 years that you really don't want to have lunch together? When you are a man and you've eaten that second meal of the day alone most of your entire married life, you develop a few habits that are hard to break. And my wife, who shares a significant DNA strain with Emily Post and Miss Manners, would never understand. This was a recipe for trouble.

That first day, Mary Ellen wanted to have lunch around noon. I usually sit down sometime between 10:30 and 4:15. Actually, I've never sat down for lunch at home in my life. I make something while standing at the fridge, then eat it on the way upstairs to watch CNN. By the time I reach the TV, I'm pretty much done eating. I just have to wipe the mustard off the banister.

Mary Ellen made it clear that a healthy meal includes a green vegetable. But you can't effectively walk up a flight of stairs eating spinach salad without a plate and a fork. Heaven knows, I've tried.

She also said she looked forward to having a conversation while we dined. I love my wife; I enjoy talking to her. But not on a Wednesday in broad daylight. And I'm sorry, but no real man has ever picked up the phone at home at 12:30 p.m. and said: "Can't talk now, Elliot, I'm dining."

Mary Ellen prepared a nutritious meal—a sauteed chicken dish with fresh broccoli. Once we were seated, she said, "Bon appetit," which is considered an affectation even in France if it's said before six at night. Then she noticed what I was wearing.

"I can't believe you have on sweats and a dirty T-shirt. Please don't sit down for a meal with me looking like that."

I was hoping she would say that. I stood straight up, grabbed my plate and headed for the stairs. A few minutes later, I heard Mary Ellen scream for me. She wasn't angry. It was my turn to clear the table.

Life at the Cellular Level

My father used to hold his hand up next to his face and flap his thumb and four fingers together to mimic my mom's incessant yakking on the phone. My wife is different from my mother. Mary Ellen does not talk much on the phone. Not that she doesn't try.

The problem started after I replaced the phones in the kitchen and living room about three years ago and added a second line. When I call the house to speak to Mary Ellen all I hear is a series of clicks, an occasional "huh?" and then a dial tone. I try back on our second line. Same thing. Later, when I arrive at the house, we have the identical conversation every time . . .

"Mary Ellen, why didn't you answer the phone?"

"I tried, but I never know what line you're calling on."

"It's the one that lights up."

"Since when?"

"Since the spring of '08."

"Well, I always hit line one, then line 2, just in case."

"Don't you see, when you hit line 2, it disconnects you from line 1?"

This seemed to fluster my wife, who continued to maintain that I had installed a system that was far too complicated for the Wolfsies, the proof being that by my own admission this was called a hard-line phone. Apparently a little too hard.

To combat this problem, I began calling Mary Ellen only on her cell phone. No answer. Then 10 seconds later my cell rings . . .

"Dick, I saw that you just called."

"I don't want you to see that I called, I want you to hear that I am calling and then answer it. Maybe if you had a little more practice at home."

"Are these the same people who make the phone in the living room? Wait, maybe I'm missing an app."

"You don't need an app to answer your phone. I may have to write a column about this."

Boy, was that the wrong thing to say. The next day, Mary Ellen made a list of all the stuff I can't master.

"Let's see, you have no idea how to open the car door with that little remote on your keychain. You click to open the passenger side door for me but all you do is double-lock all the doors; then you click again and only your door opens. Then the windows lock and the alarm goes off. I know this isn't easy. You've only had that car six years."

"Is there more?" I asked.

"How about that TV remote? You stand in front of the set and hit every button: CABLE, ON, POWER, DVD, ALL. The TV sort of comes half on, then the DVD tray opens, then everything goes black, so you push all the buttons again. Then you walk out of the room like you do at work when you screw up the Xerox machine.

"Anything else, dear?"

"You still don't know how to turn off the toaster oven, so you just yank the plug out of the wall. And that microwave must be a real stumper because I've caught you running your fingers over the control panel like it was a Ouija board. And finally, "Tear Here" doesn't mean "tear there," or "tear nearby." The words "slash with a knife" are not visible anywhere on your package of baloney.

I think she had more to say, but I couldn't bear to listen. If you'd like to hear more, give her a call. On line 2. Good luck.

Gifted Wife

It was time to pick out a few Christmas gifts for Mary Ellen, so I figured I'd select the goofiest and most impractical things I could find. Why shouldn't I? When she rips open the packages under the tree, I know what she'll say: "What were you thinking?" Exactly! It's the *thought* that counts.

I decided to steer clear of most other catalogs. Solutions, Lands' End and Eddie Bauer all ended up in the trash un-perused. However, it's hard to ignore Hammacher Schlemmer. True, I have no need for heated plantar fasciitis slippers, a wrist-wrap fish finder, or a lunch box banana protector, but those all seemed like dandy holiday gifts. And really, what says happy holidays more than a personalized diamond-tipped micro-dermabrasion kit? Here are a few other gift ideas that caught my eye . . .

The Magic Wand Remote: You program various motions into the wand so it will control the TV. Wave it in a circle and you change channels; tap it to pause the video; flick it up and down to adjust the volume. Be careful not to skewer the cat.

The Room Tidying Pickup Robot: This is an electronic mini-maid that rolls along the carpet and picks up clutter around the house. It looks like an alien, so in addition to its guarantee, it comes with immigration papers, a green card, and forms to notify the IRS.

The Dogbrella: Just when your canine buddy was feeling comfortable in his raincoat and booties, Hammacher Schlemmer came up with a better idea. With your own umbrella high above your head, use your free arm to lower the small water-diverting canopy over your Yorkie. The contraption is 100 percent clear polyethylene so that both of you can see how stupid you look.

The Pet Ramp Staircase: After years of jumping on and off the couch, your poor little canine pal has developed arthritis in his senior years. So here's a great idea: For $49.95 you can get a carpeted ramp to make your $3,000 sofa handicap-accessible for your incontinent pooch.

The Pump-Action Marshmallow Blaster or the Double-Barreled Marshmallow Crossbow: Get them both now before the Democrats pass toy gun control legislation. Completely harmless, unless marshmallows are toasted and contain a hot sticky center. Not recommended at airport checkpoints or diabetes support group meetings.

The Giant Inflatable NFL Player: It's 60 inches high and all polyester. It inflates in minutes and crouches in a three-point stance. This is the perfect gift for the woman who has no one else giving her a gift.

The 50-Foot Snowball Launcher: This device blasts perfectly round, cold, packed projectiles into your kid's back or your neighbor's face at about 40 mph. One more way to say how much your loved ones mean to you.

The Complete Swiss Army Knife: The ideal gift for Mary Ellen, who at any moment in her busy day could reach into her purse for immediate access to a fish scaler, hook disgorger, toothpick or cigar cutter. Over 200 tools and only $1,400.00. Can Christmas come soon enough?

I accidentally left the catalog on the kitchen table with all the selected items circled, knowing Mary Ellen would be accidentally snooping around to see what gifts I was planning to get her. I'm wondering now if I shouldn't dig out that Victoria Secret catalog. At least Christmas morning when she asks, "What were you thinking?" I'd have a really good answer.

Grand Vacation

The Wolfsies have returned from a weeklong vacation to the Grand Canyon. It's the only place in America where you're allowed to drag your kid to the precipice of one the world's deepest chasms, but they put you in the slammer if you feed a squirrel.

Any aspirations our small family had about making the descent to the bottom were squashed when I went into a gift shop on the South Rim. I asked the clerk to recommend a book about this National Park. Hold onto your hat—actually, hold onto anything you can. The number one seller is: *Over the Edge: Death in Grand Canyon*. What a charming choice for fans of light summer reading.

The authors do not restrict their colorful travelogue to unscheduled plunges to the bottom. They want you to know that with a little bit of poor planning, you can also die of dehydration or starvation. Rattlesnake bites, driving off the edge and eating poisonous plants are more fun options to choose from.

Writers Myers and Ghiglieri want you to know how safe the Canyon is *if* you are careful, but the book seems oddly misplaced in the gift shop so close to, well, the edge. There aren't pamphlets relating the history of scaldings on the counter of McDonald's or brochures about whimsical power tool mishaps attached to your chain saw purchases. I'm glad they didn't think of this unique marketing gimmick when the Pinto was hot (so to speak).

There are many entertaining chapters in the book: bear attacks, drownings, and rock slides, to name a few. So many ways to buy the farm and still enjoy the grandeur of nature. Maybe I'm an optimist but I look at it this way: only a few hundred deaths in six million years. That's not a bad record.

You want to hear more, don't you? In one touching chapter a man makes tea for his wife out of a deadly canyon flower and they both die within minutes. In another section, a woman tries to pet a mountain lion. There's clearly a fine line between bad luck and stupidity. Then there's the elderly couple who got lost in their 1996 Taurus on a back road. They were found dehydrated, but still alive. They had no water, but a week's supply of Depends. I'd call that ironic.

The chapter on suicide makes it clear this really is *the* place to go if you have a flair for the dramatic. It is rumored that one guy who met his maker by driving off a cliff had complained at the gate that the entry fee was exorbitant and he would never come back again. No idle threat there.

Travelers from abroad love the Grand Canyon. Europeans winter in Arizona. Asians summer in the Canyon. Americans usually fall there. About 600 feet. That's just an average, though; your actual plummet may vary.

The beauty of the Grand Canyon is overwhelming and we really did have a great time. When we left, I packed the trunk full of water and drove slowly along the winding roads, our GPS leading the way. I enjoyed that book, but I didn't want to be in the second edition.

Gray Zone

We were ready to leave our favorite but Mary Ellen was stalling. She had been fussing with her purse and made a couple of extra trips to the ladies' room.

"Let's go," I said. "I want get home by 8:30 so we don't miss *30 Rock.*"

"Dick, we can't leave yet. If we go back to the house now, we'll be in the gray zone. You know how I hate the gray zone."

On most evenings Mary Ellen pulls into our driveway about 6:30, enters the house, turns on the network news and plays with the cat. She then takes off her professional business apparel—clearly not suitable for a three-hour stint of TV crime dramas—and slings on an old pair of jeans or sweats along with a flannel shirt. By 10:00, a good night's sleep is on the radar, requiring a change into her cuddly PJs. She may watch a re-run of *Law and Order* in her sleeping garb before getting into bed with a good book.

That's the routine. It seldom varies. But wait! On that particular evening we were going to arrive home from the restaurant somewhere between 8:30 and 9:00. Yes, that is the gray zone she was fretting about. The question: Is it worth going through the second clothing change or does one get directly into sleep attire? It's not as sticky an issue as establishing peace in the Middle East, but it does pose a quandary.

I never face this predicament. Unlike my wife, whose career requires dressing like a grownup, I spend most of the day working in my basement home office, snapping the elastic band on my gray sweat pants and wiping mustard stains off my Bill Belichick pullover. Nevertheless, I'm tempted to get "sleep ready" way before my wife arrives home. "Why are you dressed for bed?" Mary Ellen will inquire when she walks in the house.

"I got ready a little early."

"I'd feel a lot better if you put your jeans back on. Otherwise, when we sit down for dinner, I'll feel like I'm visiting you at the assisted living facility. I'm not ready to start thinking about that yet."

"Why don't you put on your pajamas, too, Mary Ellen?"

"What if someone rang the doorbell, Dick? What would the neighbors say about us if they thought we got ready for bed before *Wheel of Fortune*? We might as well head out to MCL in our slippers."

She had a point. Lounging around in a robe at dinnertime may have made Hugh Hefner an icon, but it was going to wreck my reputation in the neighborhood. I did wonder who else wrestled with this issue. I called my friend Bob that night, in the middle of the gray zone, about 8:00.

"Bob, this is Dick. What are you wearing?"

"Wow, you get weirder every day, don't you?"

Bob didn't really relate to this problem. Nor did most of my friends who I tried to explain it to. I did a little Googling. Not one support group. There's a lot of denial out there.

Right now Mary Ellen is on her way home and I don't want her to know I've been in my pajamas all day. I'm going to put on my jeans, so I can put my pajamas back on in a couple of hours. This is more stress than a high-powered job. Maybe we should all retire early.

Habitual Problems

Every marriage needs a little bit of an edge. I don't want Mary Ellen and me to end up like our friends the Rodmans, who up until their 27th wedding anniversary couldn't keep their mitts off each other, but when they got back from celebrating in the Bahamas they sued each other for divorce. They were so happy, they didn't realize how miserable they really were.

"I have an idea, Mary Ellen. This evening, I'll act out all your bad habits. And you can act out all of mine. That way we'll both get a better picture of how much we annoy each other. That will add a little spice to our relationship."

I jotted down a few of Mary Ellen's little peculiarities. I didn't want to overdo it because I knew what a challenge it was going to be for my wife to create a comparable list. That night, after I returned from playing golf, Mary Ellen arrived home. She began by not shutting the door behind her so that every fly and bug could get into the house. She also tracked a lot of mud in on her shoes, but she wiped her feet on the throw rug.

Before she kissed me hello, she went upstairs and put on CNN to see what annoying things Bill O'Reilly was saying. After surfing six other channels, she came downstairs, but she left the TV on in the bedroom so I could hear it throughout the house.

Then she popped open a can of beer and guzzled it. What ran down her chin, she wiped off with her sleeve. Then she put on the living room TV, so now we could hear both sets at the same time. Finally, she kissed me hello, told me she had done nothing all day but play golf and then asked what I had made for dinner. Before I answered, she broke open a box of Pop Tarts, ate half of one, then stuffed the other half back in the box and left it on the counter. Then to nail me on my most annoying habit, she searched every room in the house pretending she lost her cell phone.

Now it was my turn to be Mary Ellen. First, I took all the plates and glasses in the sink and put them in the dishwasher, but not before I rearranged all the dirty utensils and put them in the proper compartments. Then I turned off all the lights throughout the house that had been left on all day. I went upstairs and put on pair of sweat pants and an old flannel shirt, just like Mary Ellen does. Next I came downstairs and went through the mail, carefully opening each letter, throwing away the advertisements and meticulously putting the bills in a stack.

Suddenly, I was out of ammunition. Worse, I was shooting with a pistol; my wife was packing a Gatling gun. This wasn't nearly the fun I thought it was going to be? I sat down on the couch a little depressed. My wife sat next to me and put her hand on my leg that was bouncing up and down. "I wish I had never come up with this stupid idea, Mary Ellen. How do you manage to live with me?"

"Oh, it's easy, Dick. You're habit forming."

Identity Crisis

When I grew up in the fifties, we didn't worry about much. My grandfather smoked a big cigar when he babysat for us; our family car didn't have seatbelts and my mother's cooking was so bad, we washed our hands *after* we ate. Other than our backyard bomb shelter in case of a nuclear attack, we recognized the world as a safe place. Sadly, things have changed.

For example, at the Wolfsie house everything has to be shredded before it goes in the garbage. My wife has this vision of marauders at the dumpster going through our trash and gathering important personal data. "Dick, I don't think we should put our cans and bottles at the curb, either. Someone could go through our recyclables to learn personal stuff about us. Then steal our identities. We should at least boil off the labels."

"So you think it would threaten our security if people up to no good knew I had a thing for canned peaches?"

To prove her point, Mary Ellen forwarded me an email from work warning people not to leave their GPS system in the car. Not because it might be stolen, but because if someone made off with your vehicle, the crook would know the addresses of all the places you've been, including your own home. The admonition

suggested that instead of logging where you live in the system, you put in a nearby gas station. This explains many of the heists at 7-11s.

My wife completely bought into this. "Don't you see, Dick? If they get your GPS, the bad guys will know where you live."

"Bad guys know where everyone lives."

"They do?"

"Yes, they drive up to a nice house and they say: "Hey, someone lives there. Let's rob it."

"And those same bad guys," continued Mary Ellen, "will also now see in your GPS all the places you've visited in the last several weeks."

"Imagine that: everyone from the common street thug to the cyber criminal will know the Wolfsies went to Red Lobster for dinner two weeks ago. That *is* creepy."

Mary Ellen was annoyed I wasn't taking this more seriously. According to her, you should also never put words like "Honey" or "Wife" in your cell phone directory.

"Why not?" I asked.

"Because, then they'll know how to reach me."

"And did you think thieves would call you at work just to chat? You're right: that can be annoying."

Totally frustrated with my insensitivity to this issue, she started peppering me with true-life stories of men like me who made light of this serious issue. Like the guy in Detroit who was at Ford Stadium enjoying a Lions game, but little did he know that his car was being stolen from the parking lot. The thief found the registration in the glove compartment, saw the guy's address, then robbed his house.

"That one I don't believe, Mary Ellen."

"Why not?"

"No one has enjoyed a Lions game in two years."

Then she told me the one about the crook who broke into a man's car while he was playing golf. He found the owner's cell phone on the seat and saw "Sweetie" on the Caller ID. So he texted the guy's wife: I LV U. R U home?" She texted back: NO, BK N 2 HRS. So the robber went to the guy's house to break in.

"Wow, that is a scary example. And so no one was home, right, Mary Ellen?

"No, his wife *was* home. Apparently, it was his sweetie who was out shopping."

I've printed out several different versions of this **story** and Mary Ellen made me shred them all before they went into the trash. I asked her if that was to protect my identity. "No," she said, "your reputation."

Mayo Zee Tongue

Certain topics inevitably lead to an argument. Religion and politics should be avoided at work and social gatherings. I have also found that it's best not to talk about your favorites on *American Idol* or *Dancing with the Stars*. But here's a topic that I had not anticipated would cause dissent in my marriage: mayonnaise.

Ketchup? Sure, there were always possibilities here for a tiff. You never hear a man say to his wife, "With all that ketchup on the burger, Sweetheart, you can't possibly appreciate the fine texture and flavor of the grain-fed beef." Women, on the other hand, will say: "If you put ketchup on my Chicken Kiev, I will rip your ruby-red tongue right out of your mouth."

Mustard? Yes, I could see an argument about mustard. Over the years I have attempted to improve most of my wife's cooking with a healthy dose of this condiment. What would her Pork Milanese have been without mustard? Uneventful. What would her Beef Bourguignon taste like without a glob of Dijon? I shudder to think. What about that sesame-encrusted salmon without a dollop of you-know-what? Yes, Mary Ellen and I have clashed over mustard.

But a fight over mayonnaise? Who would have predicted this?

It all started one morning last week when Mary Ellen was searching for the sugar in our kitchen cabinets and noticed that I had accidentally placed the mayonnaise jar in the cupboard rather than back in the fridge the night before. Such absent-mindedness is a part of nature. I have found my keys in the freezer and my cell phone in the dryer, but mayonnaise in the cupboard was apparently a capital offense.

Without the slightest hesitation, Mary Ellen tossed the jar in the garbage along with this denouement: "It's no good. We have to throw it out." I begged to differ. I couldn't accept the product's ruin in just a few hours. Look, if you can't fight off bacteria overnight, you're not worth the preservatives you're made of.

The next day, desperate for a smear on my BLT, I fished the mayonnaise out of the garbage and slathered it on my sandwich, then placed the jar in the fridge. Hours later my son unknowingly partook, this time making an egg salad sandwich. When Mary Ellen discovered what I had done, she panicked.

"Are you trying to wipe out the entire family?" she bellowed. "Why not open all the cans with bulging tops and make a nice bouillabaisse for the neighborhood block party?"

It was the angriest I had ever seen her, angrier than when I left the oven on when we went out for a short . . . vacation. It almost ruined our entire cruise. I picked up the mayonnaise jar and confirmed that my wife was correct. It did say "REFRIGERATE AFTER OPENING." But then my eye caught an 800 number on label, a hotline for people with emergency mayonnaise questions. I didn't know if I was calling a deli or New Deli, but I made the call.

"Hello, may I help you?"

"Yes, I have a question about food poisoning."

"First of all, this is the mayonnaise hotline, not the Mayo Clinic. And, yes, I know what you're going to ask. I get husbands all day long with this question. Commercial mayonnaise is loaded with acids that can kill bacteria. And the eggs used in prepared mayonnaise are pasteurized. It's perfectly safe."

"So I shouldn't throw it out?"

"Of course you should throw it out. A man can't win a mayonnaise argument."

He was right, of course. I didn't tell Mary Ellen about my phone call. It would have been Hellman's to pay.

Mugged on My Birthday

It's too late now, but I wish you would have sent my wife an email and told her what to give me for my birthday. She really needed your help. Mary Ellen says I am difficult to shop for. Last year I ended up with three dozen golf balls. Even though I requested them, it was still a surprise. I didn't expect pink.

In a desperate attempt to help her this year, I Googled: gifts for men in their 60s. Maybe there was a place on the Internet where women could communicate with each other about what must be a common dilemma.

One website was a blog where the children of people my age made gift suggestions. Here was the first comment:

The birthday party should convey to the celebrant that he or she is still loved, respected and appreciated. It should also be a reminder of the golden days of youth.

I checked my pulse. I was still breathing, although my blood pressure had hit the roof. I may be an irritant, but I don't want to be a celebrant. Not while I can still dress myself. Also, I may not have the best memory, but my youth was not golden. Stainless steel, maybe.

Their first gift suggestion had little appeal: "Why not a collage of stamps from that person's birth year, all in an attractive scrapbook? Can you think of a better present?" Yes, I can. How about a gift certificate for a colonoscopy.

There were several suggestions for personalized coffee mugs.

"What about an eye-catching cup with a list of all the famous people born on their birthday?" I thought that sounded like a good idea, so I did a little research about March 5 . . .

Tang Gonghong (Chinese weightlifter)

Jef Eygel (Belgian Basketball player)

Olusegun Obasanjo (former President of Nigeria)

Seriously, how long do you really own something special like this before someone swipes it? You put your mug down in the lunchroom and it's like leaving your Lexus running with the keys in it.

Here was another hint: a coffee mug decorated with the names of famous people who *died* on your birth date. What fun! I'm surprised Starbucks never thought of this. It seems tasteless, but it's nothing compared to their scones. I checked the extensive list provided for March 5. The following people all bought the farm on my special day. How festive that would look on my breakfast table next to the Metamucil.

Jay Silverheels (Tonto on the *Lone Ranger*)

Patsy Cline (country singer)

William Powell (movie star)

That list depressed me, so I thought I'd ask them to add Joseph Stalin. I'm not sure when the Soviet dictator died, but no one is going to check and **you** do need something to brighten up the mug.

The other night we went to Cracker Barrel and I saw my wife eyeing one of those little books on the gift rack that features news and statistics about the date you were born. The top of the stand starts with 1985 and the years work their way down. By the time my wife reached my year, she was on her knees. There were a few books for older people even lower on the shelf. Once the 4:00 dinner special was over, the floor was going to get very crowded.

So what did I get from my wife? The best gift was the coffee mug that says:

TO MY FAVORITE
SEXAGENARIAN

I don't like being in my 60s, but that does make it sound like a lot more fun than it really is.

All Puckered Out

No polling data is offered. No experts are quoted. No international study referenced. The people at Dentyne come flat out and say it in their newest TV commercial: The average person spends 20,000 minutes in their lifetime kissing. Again, this is simply an average. Your smooching may vary depending on whether you attend a lot of Greek weddings or have more than 15 grandchildren.

I'm not an overly competitive person, but I do believe in keeping up with the Joneses, who, by the way, are our newlywed neighbors down the street. The Fettermans next door have been married 40 years, so I'm thinking these folks may represent a more realistic role model for me.

I assume I've been rolling along at an acceptable rate up until now, but why not increase my output so my obit can read: Exceeded the standard kissing time by 2,000 minutes. Even my harshest critics would be forced to concede that when it came to lips, I was successful at putting two and two together.

When Mary Ellen came home the other night, I gave her the customary hello, but I realized that if I lingered a few seconds longer in the osculation and then multiplied that time by my predicted life span, I could increase my total production by 20 percent. Osculation, by the way, is the scientific name for kissing. Don't use that word during romantic encounters. It'll have a negative impact on your lifetime total.

After 30 years of marriage, my wife became instantly aware that I had breached the unwritten rule for time spent on the customary "Hi, honey, I'm home from work" kiss.

"What was that all about?" she asked.

"Is something wrong?"

"Your kiss. There was this delay. You were loitering on my cheek. You do know it's only Thursday."

The question, of course, is how they ever came up with 20,000 minutes. I did a little math and it looks like if your kissing career spans 75 years, you need to kiss about 47.4 seconds a day to reach this goal. I'm a happily married guy, but there are a couple of days a week that to reach this number I would have to count my relationship with the dog (we're just best friends, I assure you) and my new Big Bertha three wood that gets a little extra lovin' whenever I don't hit a ball out of bounds.

Dentyne has a Facebook page where customers put their kissers right online, revealing true-life stories about kissing. About 12,000 individuals are seeking advice on how to inform loved ones about their halitosis. Actually, it's only 11,258 people. The rest are Beagles, Cocker Spaniels, St. Bernards and the like, put off by humans who insist on going nose-to-snoot without first freshening their breath.

The Facebook site also notes: "You kiss 20,000 minutes in your lifetime. What about the other 40 million moments?" Great. It's bad enough I'm obsessed with maintaining oral hygiene while puckering, but now I find there are a slew of other situations where my breath should be pristine. I wish they had been more specific.

In order for my wife and me to someday reach the national average, I'm really going to need her full cooperation. Last night I told Mary Ellen how beautiful she is and how great dinner was. I think I have a chance of reaching that 20,000 mark, as long as kissing up counts.

Salad Confessing

I told a lie to my wife. A whopper, really. I am still not sure I got away with it. I'm a bad fibber and Mary Ellen is quite perceptive, so it's unlikely she bought it. If she did believe me, reading this will be the first time she finds out the truth. No problem. She never buys my books.

Here's what happened. My son graduated from college and moved back home. We're encouraging him to go out on his own, but with the job market the way it is, we could be looking at a couple of decades of his residing in the basement storage area, since his old room became my home office. Part of the new living arrangement is that Mary Ellen, Brett and I alternate nights to prepare dinner.

Brett has produced some tasty meals. He whipped up an awesome beef stroganoff, a respectable platter of salmon cakes and a tasty pasta primavera. We should have never let him leave home.

I have always been a failure in the kitchen. When I have an overflowing anxiety about something, my performance is hampered and the results are disappointing. Last Monday, I disappointed everyone with a pathetic pot roast, so I needed a sure-fire way to redeem myself.

The first thing I did was buy a pound of this scrumptious shrimp salad from a gourmet shop in my neighborhood. That was only the beginning of my ruse. I bought some additional frozen shrimp and stuck them in the fridge, in plain sight. Then I left a bottle of balsamic vinegar on the counter, and lined up a few stalks of half-chopped celery on the cutting board. I also put some mixing bowls in the sink and filled them with soapy water. I took two large wooden spoons, slathered them with mayo and then partially rinsed them off. This mess had my name all over it.

The sham took me an hour to pull off, about 20 minutes longer than it would have taken to make it from scratch. Of course, it would have been a lousy shrimp salad and anyone can make a lousy shrimp salad. It takes talent to pretend you made a great shrimp salad.

When Mary Ellen got home that night she surveyed the kitchen. "Well, it looks like you've spent all day in here," she said. Perfect.

Moments later we all sat down to eat. I watched as she took her first bite. "Dick, this tastes like you bought it somewhere." I was never so insulted in my life. Or was I flattered? I had to quickly ascertain the meaning of the remark. Here were the possibilities:

> I hadn't fooled her. She caught me. Yikes!
> I fooled her. But it tasted awful, like from the Target deli counter. Yuck!
> I fooled her. And it was delicious, like I got it at an expensive seafood restaurant. Yum!

Brett began spearing dark, BB-sized things out of the salad and flicking them onto his napkin. “Dad, what are these nasty-tasting doodads?”

“Well, Brett, as any gourmet cook knows . . . those are . . . we call them . . .

Thank goodness, my wife broke in. “They’re capers, Brett. Just one of the 5 or 6 exotic ingredients in this shrimp salad, about 5 or 6 more than were in your dad’s pot roast.

By now, I was sure I had been caught, but I had to ask her point blank. “Mary Ellen, honestly what did you think about my contribution this week?”

“It was fine, Dick, perfectly fine. Maybe a little fishy.”

Special Memories

"Any mail?" my wife called out from upstairs when she heard the front door close behind me.

"Just bills. Oh, wait—here's a card from the Applebaums."

"What does it say?"

"It says "Happy Anniversary."

"How thoughtful, but why are they sending it to us? Our anniversary isn't until June 14."

She came downstairs and we looked at each other in amazement. "What's today?" I asked Mary Ellen.

"I don't know. June something."

"Can't be. Wasn't it June something, yesterday?"

I made a dash to my desk and opened my appointment book. I knew it was Saturday. But which Saturday? I looked at Friday's

page. It said GOLF in bold black letters. No help—I play golf every Friday. I looked at Thursday and it was blank because I do nothing every Thursday. Wednesday was my best clue. It said dental appointment/tooth extraction. I searched the back of my mouth with my tongue. I felt I had the right week. To be sure, I ran downstairs and grabbed a newspaper. Huh? It said June 6. Wait, maybe that was last week's paper. Then I looked at the date on my watch. Even I knew January 4 wasn't right. It's been January 4 for seven years. Finally, I opened my trusty cell phone and clicked a button. Yup, June 13. And I think I took a photo of myself by mistake, to boot.

That was the good news. The bad news was that June 14 was the next day . . . our anniversary.

"Dick, we both forgot a very special day. This is unforgivable."

"Well, it wasn't what you'd call a *big* anniversary. Just the 28th."

"The 29th, actually. Now, I'm really depressed."

Mary Ellen and I sat down and tried to remember what we had done on each anniversary since we were married in 1980. It was an exercise to see if we were still as sharp as we were in the old days. We went backwards from 2008 and were doing well until we hit the early '90s.

"What did we do for our anniversary in '91, Dick? I can't remember."

"Wasn't that the year your sister came to stay with us for the week?"

"I don't have a sister. I thought that was your sister. How about '89, Dick? Now that was the year we got a bottle of Champagne and picnicked in the park."

"That doesn't sound remotely familiar, Mary Ellen."

"Sorry, maybe that wasn't you in '89; I think it was Gary in '79."

"Hey, I remember '88. That was when we rented a video, bought some popcorn, curled up on the couch and waited for the ball to drop."

"That was New Year's Eve, Dick. And you fell asleep."

"I don't know why they can't do that falling ball thing around 8:45."

All this reminiscing made Mary Ellen more unhappy. I explained that we didn't forget when our anniversary was. We simply forgot when June 14 was.

My impeccable logic seemed to soothe her. We know our relationship is strong and we both still believe our memories are as clear as ever. We do have one question, though.

Who the heck are the Applebaums?

Stop, You're Killing Me

I was working at home late one afternoon when the phone rang. My wife's cell number popped up on the caller ID, so I picked it up and said, "Hello, Mary Ellen?"

"I adore you."

How odd. My wife is a loving person, but she is not given to dreamy declarations on her way home from work. And yet, she added, "Sometimes I can't get through a minute without thinking about those romantic times we had in Rio, Fernando."

Ahhh . . . what could be more romantic than Rio? But there was a problem: I've never been to Rio. Of course, I don't have the best memory in the world. I once slept through France on a bus tour so I still swear I've never been to Paris. Also, this Fernando reference was going to be an annoying distraction for me the rest of the day.

I kept listening: "While my husband is still alive, we will never find happiness. We have to get rid of him. Soon."

As you can imagine, I found this disconcerting. It gave me the creeps when Lana Turner said it to John Garfield in *The*

Postman Always Rings Twice. However, I didn't want to jump to any conclusions. My wife has a delicious sense of humor; maybe she was just having some fun—you know, pretending she had a boyfriend and that they were going to ice me.

Then I heard a man's voice: "You are the brightest star in my galaxy, the cherry on my cake, the rose in my garden."

Now I was really getting annoyed. It was bad enough my wife wanted me eliminated, but being killed with clichés was not how I wanted my life to end.

I hung up the phone, torn about what to do. Should I confront her with what I had overheard or ignore it, hoping that maybe a movie and dinner at Cracker Barrel one night would make her realize I was worth keeping around.

That night when Mary Ellen got home, I let her know I was aware of her desire to have me whacked. I had to be subtle. "Mary Ellen, you are the brightest star in my galaxy, the cherry on my cake, the rose in my bouquet."

"I'm so embarrassed. How did you hear that?"

"You must have accidentally hit the speed dial button on your cell phone and when I picked up, I overheard the conversation in your car. How long has this been going on?"

"Since August 5th. I was trying to end it, but you know hard that can be. Once you start something, you feel like you've got to finish it. I'll have to pay the penalty."

"You're certainly cavalier about the whole thing. How much longer do you see this continuing?"

"Not much longer. My book on tape was supposed to be returned to the library a few days ago. It is such a trashy novel, but I have enjoyed it."

That's pretty much the end of the story. I'm glad Mary Ellen doesn't want to liquidate me, but she is hurt that I was so suspicious of her behavior. So far, I haven't been man enough to say I'm sorry.

As of the following Monday, the apology and the tapes were a week overdue.

Talking Trash

"What is this?" Mary Ellen asked me as she dangled a doodad in front of my face. It was small, white, plastic, hexagonal in shape, and had several grooves. "It looks like it goes to something," she said.

"I don't know what it is," I responded, which I prayed would end the discussion, but I knew it wouldn't because my wife can't leave a thingamajig alone. She has to know what it's for.

"Put it somewhere in case we ever need it. It looks important."

"So you want me to keep it because we don't know what it is for?"

"Exactly."

"Of course, if we did know what it was for, we'd also keep it. So, I guess we keep everything."

"Don't be silly, some things don't go to anything. We can throw those things away. We only keep things that look important."

I knew exactly what she meant. I have an entire drawer filled with things that look important. Not that I will ever really need them.

I decided it was time to clear out the mess that had accumulated in my office over the years. Why not begin with Mary Ellen's doodad? I was 100 percent certain that nothing in our house required anything quite like that. But there was only one way to really be sure that it was not important, that it didn't go to anything. I'd throw it away.

I tossed it in the wastebasket next to my desk and listened as it nestled to the bottom and came to rest with an audible thud. I knew I had a small window of opportunity left to retrieve it if necessary: two days before I emptied the office wastebasket in the garage receptacle; then another day before the sanitation department picked up all the week's trash. That gave me some time to rescue the thing when the inevitable happened and I realized I had thrown away something important that went to something.

A few days later, I heard the familiar sound of the garbage truck pulling away. Whatever that thing was, it was now gone forever. Just a matter of time now before I found out what it was for. The next day . . .

"Dad, Mom wants me to mount the kitchen phone on the wall. She said she thinks you have the doohickey that does that. Do you know where it is?

"Yes, on the far south side—at the city dump."

"You threw that away? Dad, didn't you know that it went to something?"

Yes, I knew it went to something. I just didn't know what it went to."

"Great, now it went to the dump?"

I headed upstairs. I removed the drawer from my desk, flipped it over and dumped the entire contents into the wastebasket: wooden knobs, old keys, pen tops, dozens of multi-colored plastic thingies, metal gizmos in various shapes and a rubber whatchamacallit with a hole in the middle. Within days, I would know the purpose of each item.

“What’s going on up there?” screamed Mary Ellen when she heard the thunderous clatter.

“Nothing,” I said. “It’s not important . . . yet.”

Way Out West

My wife is concerned about me. She thinks I don't have enough to do to keep my brain active.

"Instead of those silly TV shows you watch all day and night, why don't you try the Turner Classic Movie channel. Get some culture."

"You know how bad I am with movies. I can never follow the plot. And you won't be sitting next to me to help."

"Tomorrow night I'll be out late and *High Noon* with Gary Cooper is on at 10:00. It was an Oscar-winning performance. You'll enjoy it."

"I don't know. I'd be nervous about watching an entire Western without my favorite sidekick."

"Dick, Westerns are easy to understand. The plots are simple. You have the good guys and the bad guys. I'd prefer that you watched *High Noon* instead of those ditzy reality shows you usually pick."

I turned on *High Noon* at 10 p.m. The movie opens with a church wedding. I was starting to get a little bored during the "I do's" and then I remembered that TNT was featuring a *Law and Order* mini-marathon so I switched over for a few minutes to be sure I had already seen the episode they were showing.

Then I remembered *The O'Reilly Factor* was on and I wanted to see who Bill was telling to shut up. I watched for about five minutes, got bored and decided to check out the Golf Channel, to see a little of the replay from earlier in the day.

I went back to *High Noon* for a couple of minutes and Gary Cooper was trying to convince some guys in town to become deputies, but they weren't really interested and neither was I so I flipped over to a re-run of *Everybody Loves Raymond* so I could hear Marie zing Debra just once.

Then I switched back to *High Noon* and these two women were getting on a train to leave town—I had no idea why—and then I realized it was 11:00 p.m. and I never miss the first few minutes of *The Daily Show* so I flipped to Comedy Central.

I got caught up in that show for longer than I meant to, but I didn't want to miss any more of *High Noon* so I turned back and there were a whole bunch of dead bodies on the street, which kind of bothered me, so I switched to a *CSI* re-run where there was only one dead body at a time. I watched that for a while, but then it was 11:30 and I never miss Jay Leno's opening so I clicked on NBC.

After the monologue, he had some zoo guy with animals so I switched back to *High Noon* just in time to see Gary Cooper throw down his badge in disgust and head out of town with his wife.

Wow, what brought that on?

When my wife got home, I told her the movie was okay, but that I thought the plot was hard to follow. That ended any chance I'd ever again choose *Turner Classic Movies*. I sure hope there's something else on.

Wife On Call

My wife's cell phone keeps calling me. She's not calling me—just the phone. We are fairly certain we did not pay for this feature, but my bill is complicated, so it's hard to tell.

Here's how it works. Or doesn't work. I'm at home minding my own business when suddenly I hear the William Tell Overture. No, it's not the Lone Ranger on the line. I check the number and it's my wife, I assume contacting me from work to remind me to take three tilapia filets out of the freezer and defrost them. This could be the most exciting call I get all day.

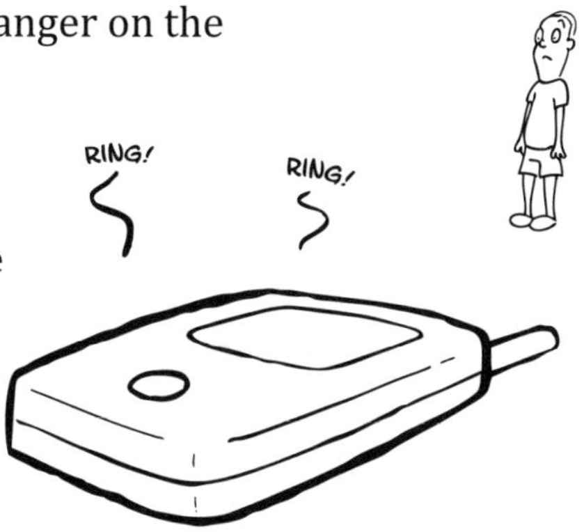

But as I said, it's not Mary Ellen. Apparently her cell phone has been jostled in her purse and somehow redialed the last caller, which was my number. So I pick up and I hear my wife talking—not to me—but on her office phone. I really don't want to spy, but for 30 years of our relationship she has accused me of not listening to her. I'm always looking to improve my marriage.

Nothing interesting going on in that first ten minutes. Mary Ellen was typing on her computer and I was hoping that a missttroke or two might elicit a few mild expletives that I could tease her about that night. "Oops!" did not give me much material to work with.

I listened in on Mary Ellen's office activity until almost noon when suddenly the room went silent. She must have decided to have lunch at her desk, probably the clam chowder she brought from home. Think about this. She's completely alone in her office eating a bowl of soup, but she never slurps. Why is this not on her resume?

My biggest disappointment was my wife's professionalism. When she talked with her colleagues it was always strictly business, which is why when she gets home at night she tells me what a busy day she had. The people I've worked with over the years know how to slack off. They know that if a third of their day isn't spent on office gossip, leafing through *People* magazine, or playing solitaire on their cell phone, they're headed for an early ulcer.

This rare opportunity to eavesdrop had not afforded me any real dope to use against my wife. Instead, maybe I could win some brownie points with the help of the cell phone. I went to get a haircut and called Mary Ellen. Right before she picked up, I stuffed the phone in my pocket so the muffled sound would make it appear as though my phone had also accidentally called her at work.

"You know, Buddy, as I sit here having my hair cut I'm reflecting on how lucky I am. I have the most incredible woman: beautiful, intelligent, sensitive. Without her, my life would be lonely and without purpose . . . "

It was the perfect ruse, but I hadn't planned on my barber being such a wise guy. "Yes, you are a lucky man to have such a woman, Dick. I sure hope your wife doesn't find out."

I fumbled for the phone in my pocket, but it was too late.

Mary Ellen had hung up. I panicked. I tried calling her back to explain but she didn't answer. She knew Buddy was a jokester—she's seen my haircuts. Later that night I tried to talk to her.

"Not now, Dick. I want to watch *Desperate Housewives*. We'll talk another time."

"When?"

"I don't know. Why don't you have your phone call my phone?"

MOPEY ABOUT EVERYTHING ELSE

Slice of Life

I don't usually have my meals delivered to me.

My pizza restaurant of choice is only five minutes from the house, so it's not a big deal. I figure that if I'm going to wolf down six or eight slices of pure cholesterol, I should at least get some exercise by driving a couple of blocks.

It was a snowy night, so I parked myself in front of a roaring fire and decided to arrange for a speedy dinner drop-off. "Hello, Donatos, I'd like to order two medium pizzas for my family. One with sausage and one with pepperoni and mushroom."

"Do you have any coupons, sir?"

"Yes, but they are all for a different pizza chain and they expired in June of '05."

"Not a problem. What major intersection are you near?"

"We're just south of 86th and Mud Creek."

"One moment, sir. I'll have to talk my supervisor about this."

Then, a long silence. Finally, the boss picked up the phone. "Sir, this is Eugene, the manager. I've been doing some checking, and I have some bad news for you."

"Look, if you're out of pepperoni, I can get through this. I'm tough. How about meatball, instead?"

"It's not that. It's more serious. This is difficult to say, sir, but according to MapQuest, you live in a pizza dead zone.'"

"What does that mean, 'pizza dead zone'? I feel like I'm talking to Rod Serling."

"Well, there are four of our pizza chains within 10 minutes of you, but you aren't in the delivery area for any of them. Pizza-wise, sir, you are nowhere. Pizza non grata, so to speak."

"Well, of all the luck. Not only am I a liberal who accidentally moved into a neighborhood represented by Congressman Dan Burton, but now I've also been gerrymandered out of pizza delivery. What can we do about this, Eugene?"

"You could meet the truck at the edge of the dead zone. Do you know where the stop sign is at the intersection of . . . "

"This is ridiculous. I get my newspaper delivered every morning. The Girl Scouts and the Jehovah's Witnesses never have a problem finding my front door. I even know the UPS guy on a first-name basis. If Brown can do something for me, why can't Donatos Pizza?"

"Look, sir, I can't make any exceptions. If I let you order a pizza for delivery, the next thing you know, the people next door to you will be ordering pizzas. Then the whole neighborhood will want pizza delivered from us. We don't have time for that. We're trying to run a business here."

"OK, Eugene, suppose, just suppose, I wanted to order 100 pizzas with all the toppings. Then would you deliver to me?"

"You mean, ask my employees to enter the dead zone? In good conscience, I don't think I could do that."

"Eugene, this is a subdivision in Castleton. Not the Bermuda Triangle."

"Sir, I've just called up some research while we were chatting that may explain this problem from a business standpoint. The data show that if we expanded service into your area it would increase our net profit by only 1.567 percent during the week and only 2.567 percent on weekends."

"Wow, those are impressive statistics. Is that based on a mathematical extrapolation using advanced calculus?"

"No, we just use a simple pie chart."

Crash Course

A couple of local TV news spots recently have made me question what I do for a living. One station did a story on how to save money when dining out. The first tip was to order items that are less expensive. My wife was working late, but I called her at the office because I didn't want take a chance on forgetting this earth-shaking news. If I had only realized the steak and shrimp platter was pricier than the deep-fried chicken planks, who knows how much I could have saved. The station also reported that you can save money by ordering tap water instead of a triple dirty vodka martini. Why was I never told about this?

Then the other night, I saw another must-see segment about . . . are you sitting down? You better be, because the story was about the increasing number of people who end up in the emergency room—because they trip over their pets.

Sadly, the story lacked the kind of in-depth analysis that I have been trained to do as a crack reporter. Inexplicably, all pets in the study were lumped together—which makes them easier to trip over— preventing you from making an intelligent purchase at the pet store. If no one has bothered to take the time at the emergency room to record whether you stumbled over a hermit crab or an Irish Wolfhound, you're just another typically uninformed consumer looking at a bunch of useless statistics.

I have stumbled over my dog many times, and I am always struck by the look Toby gives me as I crash head-first into my oak night stand. Mark Twain once said: Even a dog knows the difference between being kicked and being tripped over. I think this is true because I know from my beagle's expression that, if he could talk, he'd be saying: "Walk much?" I once had a Cocker Spaniel that I also continually became entangled with. His expression seemed to say: "Have a nice trip?" I finally gave the pooch away. No dog of mine is going to spout clichés while my head is lodged in the mahogany credenza.

How many people trip over their pets? This year the number hit 86,000 emergency room admissions. This is already about 85,500 more than swine flu admissions, but the CDC (the Committee for Dog Collisions) has tried to conceal these numbers concerned people will hide in their bedrooms fearing their Chihuahua is lying in wait, just panting for a chance to assist you in breaking your patella.

The problem may be related to the economy. It's not only humans who are worried about the worldwide financial crisis. Many dogs are having trouble getting their 14 hours a night. They lie awake worrying about where their next meal is coming from. Canines walk the house in the dark, only to run head and leg into their owner who is pacing the halls, already upside down on his car loan, and now about to be upside down on his coffee table.

Even cats, historically uninterested in global monetary issues, seem to be getting more under-foot lately. Truth is most feline-related admissions are due to pet lovers putting one foot in the kitty litter and then doing a split worthy of a perfect score from Bruno on *Dancing with the Stars*.

I am now paranoid that my dog and cat hold secret meetings each night hashing out a devious plan to weave between my legs as I gingerly make my way up the stairs with a bagel and hot cup of coffee. No one wants to contract swine flu, but here's the truth: There is a better chance you'll trip over a potbellied pig.

The Egg and I

I'm inherently lazy, so if there's something on the market that might make my life a little easier, you can count on me to try it. That's why my interest was piqued when I saw on amazon.com the EZ Cracker, a nifty little mechanism that (the manufacturer claims) takes all the work and mess out of cracking eggs.

In the past, I've always had a good relationship with eggs. I'm an over-easy kind of guy and as a kid I really kicked butt on Easter morning. But now I was starting to worry. According to the website, breaking raw eggs on the sides of bowls and countertops has had some tragic consequences. Now, for a mere $17.95, you get a product that guarantees you will never find eggshells in your food again.

Here's how it works: You simply place the egg in this hand-held appliance and squeeze the handles. Before you know it, it has sliced the egg cleanly in half and deposited the liquid contents in a bowl, yolk intact. I'll wait while you grab your credit card.

The ad also says it will take all the drudgery out of making meals. For birthdays or anniversaries, you men out there should give this gift idea some serious consideration. Isn't your wife a little bit tired of chocolates and massage gift certificates?

Here's the best part: There is also a tiny spindle attached to this kitchen tool that you can insert into the raw egg and after a bit of witchcraft, the egg is scrambled while it is still in the shell. Why is the iPad getting all the good PR?

The website listed testimonials from recent customers, real people whose lives of egg-cracking despair had led them to this once-in-a-lifetime purchasing opportunity. Some of the buyers were pleased, but many were carping about how the razor blade in the device meant it couldn't double as a toy for their toddlers. I'm not a child psychologist, but Tickle Me Elmo sounds like a lot more fun to me.

One disgruntled woman wrote: "A huge waste of money . . . poorly designed . . . it totally mangles the egg. The edge is dangerous. I'm throwing it in the trash." I guess you can't please everyone. I wonder if she's happy with her Toyota.

Here's another complaint: "I would love to give this five stars, but I find that it doesn't work with free roaming eggs." Don't eggs have to be stationary in order for the thing to operate properly. One customer said the EZ Cracker was "okay," but that she probably wouldn't order another one. Was she thinking of putting one in the extra bedroom?

For marketing purposes, Amazon.com wants you to know about other products that were purchased by the same people who bought the EZ Cracker. Many opted for the $5.99 Egg Yolky, the state-of-the art way to divide the yellow from the white in order to make cholesterol-free dishes. I'm thinking that people too lazy to crack their own eggs are not real interested in a healthy diet.

There were other purchase options for egg lovers, including a round wire thingamajig that cuts the top off of soft-boiled eggs.

One husband was angry his wife left it out where the kids could find it because he thought it was her IUD. I wish I were making this up.

I'm going to stick to the old standard methods of food prep. What would Eggs Benedict be without a little crunch?

English Channels

When I was kid, there were a lot of rules in our house. My father had a workshop in the basement, so his list of no no's was a great deal longer than Mom's: paint thinner is not a beverage; a band saw is not a musical instrument; a blow torch is not a hair dryer.

Mom did have one rule that she was adamant about. We were never to slice a Thomas' English Muffin with a knife. Instead, the product was to be carefully pried apart with a fork, so that both halves revealed their celebrated nooks and crannies. Then a careful toasting produced the legendary ideal crunch.

As any muffin maven knows, the jagged terrain provides a nesting place for butter, cream cheese or jam. My father did not share the view that a sliced muffin is a muffin maligned. He routinely hacked away at Thomas with a kitchen knife and when Joan found the half-eaten evidence on Dad's plate, she'd scold him in front of the entire family. In retaliation, Arnie would then use the same knife to split an Oreo cookie into two cream-covered halves, a clear violation of the twist and detach rule, still operative today.

I don't know the difference between a nook and a cranny. However, I always figured that the 75-year-old recipe for this highly touted topography was a carefully guarded corporate secret, not unlike the undisclosed ingredients of Coca Cola. Or what part of the chicken a McNugget really is.

And now it has been revealed that only seven people in the world know the formula for the nooks and crannies, and one of them left the company, headed for Thomas' fierce competitor, Hostess, maker of Wonder Bread and Twinkies. Now the plot thickens, or rises—pick your bakery metaphor. Turns out that Thomas' English Muffins is currently owned by a Mexican food company, Bimbo Bakeries, which sounds like a south-of-the-border Hooters. In reality, Bimbo is one of the largest food conglomerates in the world. I think they make almost everything except frozen tacos and burritos, which they farm out to the Chinese.

Bimbo and Hostess are now in a legal battle over Thomas' recipe for nooks and crannies. Make no mistake: this has shmear campaign written all over it. In the true spirit of English muffins, both sides will be equally represented. The jury may have a tough time. I expect a split decision.

It's bad enough the Limeys are being blamed for the Gulf oil spill, but now the public will incorrectly assume this English muffin scandal is also about the Brits. If the judge lays down a nook and cranny cease and desist order, we'll have both a petroleum spill and a potential jelly leak. Petroleum and Jelly. This is a headline writer's dream.

The history of the craggy surface was anything but smooth scaling. Several notable bumps along the way perplexed the inventor, Samuel Bath Thomas, who in 1874 made the discovery after a failed attempt to find a cure for acne. Some of his early versions were disasters, including the Moon Muffin, which was all nooks and no crannies. Another early snafu was calling it Tom's English Muffins, since no one knew where to put the apostrophe. Thomas'? Thomases'? Thomas's?

The Bimbo people are always searching for ways to increase visibility. I hope they don't try to sell their products to fairgoers this summer. I love Indiana State Fair food as much as the next guy, but a deep-fried English muffin doesn't sound quite Hoosier enough for me.

Funny You Should Say That

I have only dim memories of my college years, but I do recall that I faithfully sent the required letter home to my parents each week. Phone calls were pricey and the epistle seemed a more sincere way to communicate. (This is the first time I have ever used the word epistle. And the last.)

I remember dashing off lines like, "Hi, Mom, Haven't eaten in a month, send money . . . "

"Dear Mom and Dad,
Just hypothetically, any thoughts about being grandparents?"

"Hey, Pop, got my grades. Don't worry about that expensive cap and gown rental."

Adding "Just kidding" after each of my remarks was unnecessary. It was clear to my parents that I was simply honing my jesting skills. My father was always asking me, "Are you some kind of comedian?" The answer was yes.

Lately, there has been a crisis in confidence when it comes to emailing and texting. The reason is simple: We type messages at lightning-speed, sometimes to people we don't know well. So we want to be 100 percent sure we are not misunderstood. Which is why we clarify our intent at the end of a sentence with little figures called emoticons.

The importance of these symbols was made clear by an email I received last week. "Dick, at the start of your column, my newspaper introduces you as *humorist* Dick Wolfsie. That always makes me laugh."

Couldn't the author have had the courtesy to throw in a smiley face to assist me in interpreting this message? Did he think I was funny—or not? I emailed the letter to three people to elicit their opinions and got these responses.

Heidi (my editor): Either he thinks you are really funny, or he thinks you're an insufferable bore. Just sayin'. '-)

Bob (my friend): Dick, he obviously thinks it's hysterical anyone would use the same word to describe you as they would Mark Twain :-(.

Mary Ellen (my wife): I don't think he considers you funny. I understand what he's saying. -:)

I emailed back and asked for his phone number so we could discuss this further. "Tom, this is Dick Wolfsie. I got your email and I'm a little perplexed by what you said."

"Did it come encrypted?"

"No, but I am not sure what your point is. You forgot to use those punctuation doodads. They help the reader understand the real meaning of your comments."

"Dick, I do think you are funny."

"Terrific! Thanks."

"Not so fast, Dick. I don't like funny people. They annoy me."

"Tom, I think you mean: "Funny people annoy me. Parenthesis, dash, colon?"

"What does that mean: Parenthesis, dash, colon?"

"It's a verbal emoticon. Like the smiley face people use in emails. That would tell me I don't really annoy you. You're just having some fun with me, right?

"Okay, let's try this, Dick. I read your newspaper column each week. Pound sign, infinity sign, dot, dot, dot.

"What does that mean: pound sign, infinity sign, dot, dot, dot?"

"It means that your article often feels like it's never going to end. Does that help you catch my drift?

This conversation was not going as I planned. So all I could say to Tom before I hung up was @#%^&*$. And I'm feeling really good about that :).

Keep a Lid On It

Several years ago a woman from Hollywood, Florida noticed the image of the Virgin Mary in a grilled cheese sandwich. She sold the item on eBay for $28,000. She claimed it was whole wheat, but ya gotta figure it was Wonder Bread.

I started paddling through my wife's beef stew hoping to have a similar experience with my meal, but with little success. Then I bought a package of frozen vegetables at Marsh and when I opened it up I thought, for a brief moment, that I saw Helio Castroneves in the carrot, cauliflower and green bean medley. Once the glob started to thaw, it honestly could have been any racecar driver. So I just ate it.

People who are looking for a quick buck on eBay will start imagining these culinary apparitions. It's one thing to look into the clouds and see Donald Duck; it's quite another to start telling people you saw Hanna Montana in your eggplant parmigiana.

A London newspaper recently reported that a British woman said she saw the face of Jesus in the lid of a jar of Marmite while preparing breakfast for her 4-year-old son. This is the kind of story that gives you pause. Not about why the Lord works in such mysterious ways—no, it makes you wonder what the heck Marmite is.

I Googled Marmite and I discovered that this sticky brown salty paste—known as Vegemite by many of its victims—is a glutamic acid-rich yeast extract that looks like an industrial lubricant. So why is Mom making her kid eat this crapola instead of Fruit Loops or Captain Crunch? Where are children's protective advocates when you need them?

I wondered if I would like Marmite, but then I read it was a big hit with vegetarians. That ended any potential food fest or late-night gorging for me. Maybe if I knew how Marmite was made, that would endear me to this nutritious repast. Here's what I found: "Salt is added to a suspension of yeasts, allowing the cells to shrivel. The yeast then self-destructs. Then the dying cells are heated at which point the thick hull walls must be sieved out." Yum. This makes the processing of Johnsonville Brats look good even to vegans.

Studies show that people who eat Marmite are less apt to be bothered by mosquitoes; apparently the little pests would rather suck the blood out of those who have inhaled a sack of White Castles than feed on foodies who spread Marmite on their Triscuits.

In the course of learning about yeast spreads, I also came across a list of the basic taste sensors on our tongues. The first six are: sweet, sour, salty, bitter, spicy and astringent. The astringent sensor is the mouth's way of warning the guy who staggers home at three in the morning that the funny taste in his mouth is not Pepsodent but his wife's anti-wrinkle cream.

The seventh taste we can detect, the one that best describes Marmite, is called "umami." Huh? Finding out that umami is number seven was like finding out the name of the dwarf I can never think of is Steve.

People who eat Marmite have a sense of humor. Aficionados have a favorite funny line they share at the annual Marmite soirees and conventions. Stop me if you've heard it. It's the one about the guy who won a lifetime supply of Marmite. One jar.

Not funny? Oh well, at least it wasn't tasteless.

Keep Your Chin Up

Surveys show that most people hate at least one part of their body. I'm not happy with my ears, for example. I think they stick out more than they should. My wife says I'm crazy and to be that obsessed with my own looks makes me appear very elfish. I think she meant selfish. Freud wasn't all wrong.

Every morning when I shave, I tilt my head down to look at my receding hairline. For a long time people asked me if I was losing my hair. Not really. I knew exactly where it was. In the sink. About 15 years ago, I had a hair transplant. A hair transplant is sort of like what happens when a person dies. "He's gone to a better place," people often say. That's the same with my hair. I don't have more hair, but what I had, the doctor put in a better place.

While looking in the mirror, I noticed a chin that I had not been aware of before. I was already happy with the two I already had. Fortunately, that morning I saw something advertised on TV that gave me hope. It's called The Miracle Neck Slimmer, a device they claim was created by a world-renowned physiotherapist. I was all ears.

At first, I thought the contraption was a scam, but they said that the manufacturer guarantees a 68 percent reduction in neck wrinkles. I have achieved similar results by simply slinging my head back and looking straight up at the ceiling. The results are temporary, of course, and I have slammed into several doors, but it does work. Well, I think it works. It's hard to look in the mirror in that position.

The gadget looks like one of those slap-and-chop thingies you pound with the palm of your hand to pulverize a Vidalia onion. With the Miracle Neck Slimmer, you place the apparatus under your chin, then bob your head up and down like common poultry. Springs in the device create tension. It's like your neck and chin are getting a good workout on a tiny Stairmaster. You can see why I was hooked.

You also get a luxury faux-leather carrying case that has emblazoned on it: "Miracle Neck Slimmer," which I am sure got everyone who was sitting on the fence to whip out their MasterCard. So why would you want to advertise you made this purchase? It might as well say: AARP Gift Bag.

The enclosed DVD gives you precise directions on how to properly jog your skull to and fro. It looked to me like someone auditioning to be a bobble-head doll or a back-up for the San Diego chicken. They also throw in an accelerator cream. I think it's an anti-aging lotion, but it could be an ointment to make your head go faster.

Finally, in the unlikely event you have resisted their sales pitch, they offer you a second Miracle Neck Slimmer for free. I had assumed that no matter how many chins I had, one device would be enough. Their website suggested the additional Slimmer would make an excellent gift to give to your spouse.

Gee, what could go wrong with that idea? “Mary Ellen, you know those luscious little neck wrinkles you have? Well, for just $19.95 plus shipping and handling . . . ”

At least it would be easier to see my extra chins because I’d have my head handed to me.

Lap of Luxury

I may have a disease called erythema ab igne. I had never heard of it before now. Nor, apparently, has the spell-checker on my computer. If I have the illness, the same squiggly red lines that appeared underneath those words will appear all over my legs, as well. Also a few blotches and a little mottling. I can hardly wait to take my pants off to check.

The disorder is a result of having your laptop computer rest on your lap for hours upon hours. The effect is a discoloration of your skin that is disgusting to look at and potentially dangerous. Wait, I might be confusing this with going to a tanning salon.

Erythema ab igne (EAI) was first identified by two Swiss doctors who learned that people in pricey ski chalets found it was cheaper to warm up their laps than to turn up the thermostat. The two MDs in Switzerland were thrilled to discover a new illness because the Swiss are so health conscious that even a computer virus is covered by socialized medicine.

What is interesting about this malady is that scientists also did research with youngsters who played video games up to 12 hours a day and discovered that although these kids had not overheated their legs, most of them had fried their brains.

Like most diseases, EAI is commonly referred to by a name that is easy for the lay person to remember. Doctors are calling it Toasted Leg Syndrome but I'm hoping they'll reconsider that decision. When I think of toasted, it conjures wonderful images and memories like Post Toasties and French toast. But nowadays, everything is toasted. If they snuck in Toasted Leg Syndrome on Panera's menu between the turkey and artichoke panini and the sesame bagel with seared ahi tuna, I don't think anyone would notice. And they give you chips with it.

According to the New England Journal of Medicine, there were five other technology-related mishaps over the past year, but they're not that interesting, so I made up these stupid ones:

1. A woman clobbered her husband over the head with his new HP when she realized hooker.com was not a site for golfing enthusiasts.

2. A cat in Dayton, Ohio got its tongue caught in a USB port. Now every time Molly coughs up a hairball, it's followed by six years of income tax returns.

3. A man in California hid his wife's birthday gift, a new computer, in the kids' treehouse. During a tremor, the box was rocketed across the yard and struck him in the back of the neck, proving an Apple does fall far from the tree.

4. A near-sighted accountant mistook his notebook computer for a corned beef sandwich, took one megabyte and broke his front tooth. He also double-clicked his pickle.

5. A father of nine in Utah purposely left the computer in his lap for two days because he read that prolonged heat exposure in this area could potentially lead to infertility. This seemed less scary and a lot cheaper than a vasectomy.

Update: His wife downloaded twins nine months later.

My brother in New York spends a great deal of time online. He once dozed off while emailing with the computer resting on his legs and woke up a few hours later to a searing pain. He jumped up from his recliner and starting hopping around the room. His $700.00 computer smashed onto the floor. Even for Manhattan, that's a lot of money for a lap-top dance.

Number Please

I'd like to share a few numbers with you:

4927262920202826
5736282018082727
9284748495483838

These are the tracking numbers for the Christmas gifts I bought on line last year. I then pasted the figures into the UPS or FedEx website to determine when the items would land on our doorstep.

By the way, those are not the exact numbers. I substituted bogus numerals above because I don't want you tracking my packages. If I put in a pretend phone number here, I bet you'd call it and then you'd email me saying you got some poor lady in Metamora who's about to have a nervous breakdown because her phone keeps ringing in the middle of the night. And whose fault is this?

I did a Google search to learn the terminology used to express a large string of integers, and I've discovered a whole new lexicon. We have quadrillion, quintillion, sextillion, decillion, tredetrillion, novemdecillion and vigintillion. I'm going to play this safe and just call them all gazillions. Whatever you call them, it doesn't make sense that tracking a package should require so many digits.

I'm no math wiz, but my neighbor who teaches calculus told me that those gargantuan numbers suggest that each person on the planet would receive about a million gifts. Wow. What happened to the world economic crisis? And I can tell you this: someone is going to get two million presents because I'm usually get about four packages under the tree, so I am obviously pulling down the average.

Here's another code: 783930404X9056.

That's the online pharmacy confirmation number for my cholesterol medicine. I knew there were a lot of people out there with lipid problems, but my mistake was only counting people on this planet. I also don't know that X means, but it scares the heck out of me.

We see a similar conundrum (not a word I use lightly) in other areas. My house number is 8210. No matter how many times I count the homes in my cul de sac, I usually get around four. With two glasses of Merlot, the most I see is five.

My friend Jerry works at a small company here in town. When I call his office, I get a prompt that says: For Tom, press 3056, for Jerry press 3157, for Adrian press 3021. I've been to his place of business. Where are the 3,000-plus phones? Imagine if we all got this pretentious. "Mary Ellen, it's your brother calling from Oregon."

"Which line, Dick?"

"Extension 5696."

"Huh? We only have two phone lines in this house."

"I know. I know. I just hope your brother heard me say that. How cool does that sound?"

Then there's my computer. The model number is 367. I called the company and they told me since 1984 they've manufactured about 23 versions of this desktop series, so I posed the obvious question. "Then how could this be model 367?"

"Sir, the missing numbers represent defective prototypes that didn't pass the necessary tests."

This makes me really happy that I never flew to New York on a 746.

Interestingly, the original Social Security card back in 1937 was 001-01-0001. The first recipient was Morris Ackerman whose initial check was for seventeen cents. He was simply beside himself with how generous the government was. They sure had his number.

Peanut Butter in a Jam

I recently got this note from my brother in New York:

With all the trouble in the Middle East, failing banks, businesses closing and our nation in debt, it's a good thing that some people have their eye on the really important things. He went on:

The chain Wild Wings sold 40 billion wings last year. Do the math.

I'm doing it right now. If they sold 40 billion wings, that's like, hold on . . . give me a second. WOW: that's 20 billion chickens! Well, not quite. There's Eldridge, aka Lefty, a famous chicken who lives in Mentone, Indiana. Lefty still survives because he once saved the hen house when it caught on fire by squawking and awakening the Walker family. So why does Eldridge have only one wing? "You don't eat a chicken that smart all at once," said old man Walker, who obviously spends a lot of time reading Internet jokes.

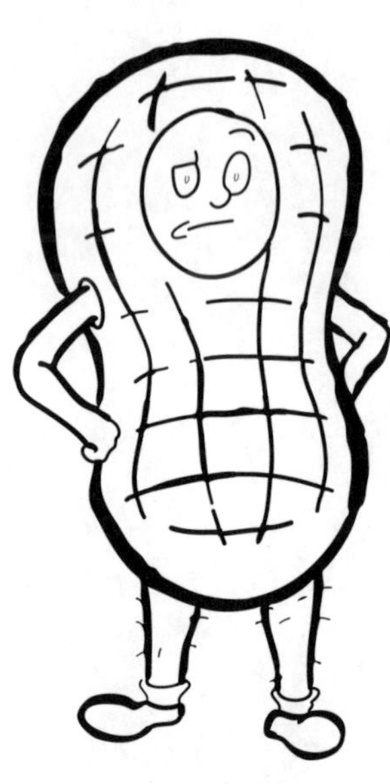

There's more bad food news every day. A few years ago there was a spinach scare. As a youngster, I was a little frightened of spinach—as are most kids. Using Popeye to sell the leafy vegetable didn't work for me. Back then, effective advertising usually involved some kind of implicit guarantee that use of the product would attract the opposite sex. As for me, a full decade before women went from a vague attraction to an obsession, I knew I was not in the market for anyone who looked like Olive Oyl.

You may recall the peanut butter scare a few years back, which became a real sticking point for Jiffy fans who see nearly everything as a sticking point. I went on this government website to read about peanut butter and salmonella (one of the few combos not endorsed by those aficionados), and was shocked to see how many hundreds of foods have been tagged as lethal. For example, there was concern about Guangdayan Brand Dried Sweet Potato and I hadn't heard a peep about it. All the Kashi Go Lean Powder Chocolate Energy Mix had been quietly hustled off the shelves. And I don't want to scare you, but the Kyosai Sengiri Daikon, better known as dried radish, caused some serious gastric problems. I'm sorry if all this information has reached you too late.

But back to peanut butter. I guess we all knew that peanut butter had a lot of peanut butter in it, but on this FDA website there was long list of products that the government said had "undeclared" peanut butter. That means that somehow, peanuts wormed their way into a factory and got into the strawberry jam or the raspberry fruit tarts without anyone knowing it . . .

"Mr. Farnsworth. This is Jensen down in security. There's someone suspicious looking down here who wants entry into our processing plant."

"Well, who is it, Jensen?"

"He says he's a federally approved additive, but between you and me, I think he's some kind of a nut."

Finally, I learned that Amy's Tofu Scramble in a Pocket Sandwich has been recalled. Apparently, this delectable treat had "undeclared milk" in it.

I understand how a peanut could sneak into a factory, but someone should have noticed that cow walking around.

Phone Ex

I thought I was having trouble selling my books. Apparently, the phone company can't even give theirs away. They're piling up in hallway closets and on doorsteps. Halloween night, witches and goblins grabbed for a Reese's Peanut Butter Cup at the Wolfsie house and then stumbled over huge a stack of phone books.

Will the White Pages survive? This is a gray area. Telephone companies claim that people who want to reach out and touch someone simply go to the Internet—right after they reach for the new phone book and put it in the recycling bin.

There are environmental issues, as well. A typical phone book weighs 3 pounds, 9 ounces, a little more than a dozen iPhones. Or, exactly the same as 3 pounds, 9 ounces of potato salad, which I think is a much funnier image. Half a billion phone books are printed each year in the United States, the product of 19 million trees. This is ironic. The best phone number I ever got in my life was carved directly into a tree.

Emily Goodman of Northwestern University is doing her doctoral thesis on the history of phone books, probably because her roommate took her first choice: "What ever happened to the doily?" Emily names 300 million people without permission in her potential page-turner, clearly a class action suit waiting to happen. Emily laments the passing of this cultural icon. "It's sort of heartbreaking," she said. This is one sensitive chick. I hope her cat never dies.

Combine the end of the phone directory with the demise of the phone booth and that means the end of late night retreating into the glass enclosure looking up and phoning people with names like Bart Simpson, James Kirk and Barney Rubble. "Hey, Barney, you are my favorite actor," or "Captain Kirk, can you tell Scotty to beam me up?" I'm sure going to miss those days.

Robert Thompson, a pop culture professor at Syracuse University, is now on AARP's hit list with this tacky observation: "Anyone who doesn't have access to a computer is probably too old to read the small print in the White Pages, anyway." This prompted his 87-year-old mother to get out her bifocals, look up her attorney's phone number, and hack little Bobby right out of the will.

No more White Pages also means the end of notoriety for three residents of the Indianapolis area. The name Aaaron (yes, three A's) will no longer have the status of being first in this soon-to-be-defunct book. I tried to call her all day last week, but her line was always busy. That's what happens when your name starts with AAA. You get lots of calls from people who drove their SUVs into a ditch or left their headlights on while they were in Walmart.

Zymbroski is the very last name in the Indianapolis phone book. The couple used to live in Toledo, which has a higher population of Polish people, so they were bested by the Zyponskis and the Zyronskis. Motivated to move down in the world, they relocated to Indy and secured their highly coveted lowly position. I called the other day to see how they felt about the news. "This is Dick Wolfsie. I wanted to talk to you about the phone directory possibly ceasing production."

"I guess you're calling us because we are the last name in the Indianapolis phone book?"

"Actually, I'm calling *everybody* in the book. I'm just glad this nightmare is finally over."

Sitting Pretty

What has happened to the art of sitting? People nowadays don't simply sit; they have to be involved in some activity like emailing, blogging, twittering, reading, or watching TV.

When I was a kid, people in my neighborhood sat on their front porch. Of course, this was New York so they were mostly protecting their valuables or waiting for the police to arrive. But they were sitting, nonetheless.

In some of those old English novels, there were sitting rooms. If you ever saw a movie or read a book about life in those days, you'd know that people also did a lot of yakking to each other while they were sitting. They would converse about the murder that recently occurred in the sewing room or speculate why the downstairs maid was spending so much time upstairs. In reality, these were talking rooms, not sitting rooms.

When you are sitting you are not wasting time. That is why we need to applaud the historical significance of this leisurely activity. For it is in this repose that the truly lazy people of the world have made their impact. Do you think it was hard-working stiffs who came up with the idea for the backhoe, the chainsaw and the snow blower? Heavens no. It was the sluggish and the indolent solving the world's problems while completely at rest.

Cracker Barrel Restaurant has the potential to bring back sitting as an art form. They have this nifty front porch chock full of sturdy rocking chairs. Rarely, however, is someone sitting in one of them. Instead, people are looking at the price tags on the arm or complaining about the 30-minute wait for the meatloaf special. Cracker Barrel customers are the perfect people for sitting. Many of them sport suspenders and dangle toothpicks from their mouths. This is sit waiting to happen.

Fewer and fewer people have front porches, the traditional place for this non-activity. Sitting alone inside your house is a little weird. You see, part of the charm of sitting is that you are publicly displaying that you have the time and the inclination to park your rear end in a chair. Not a bill to pay, a chore to do, or a place to go. You can't flaunt this in private. If word got out you were in your spare bedroom staring at the walls, the neighbors would call for some form of crisis intervention. But sit on your front step and gaze into space with a slight smirk and there is immediate neighborhood speculation about an unexpected inheritance, a hot lottery ticket stashed in your sock or you and the new UPS driver.

Sometimes to relax I go and sit in my driveway in an old beach chair and wait for my wife to get home from work. Toby, my trusted beagle, lounges next to me. No music, no book, no nothing. When my neighbor Charlie sees me he always grabs a stool from his garage and plants himself next to me. Then he wants to chat endlessly about politics or religion or why Herb shouldn't be reelected as the subdivision president. I hate to be unfriendly, but lately I've mustered up the nerve to tell Charlie I'd rather be alone.

Some people just don't sit well with me.

Soft Sell Guy

I'm a sucker for anything that might make me a better husband, so when an email appeared in my inbox with the subject: WHAT WOMEN WANT, you can be sure I clicked on it. I knew there was a chance this was an ad for something embarrassing (enough said), but there was also the possibility I was about to get valuable insight into the female psyche.

So what do women want? Apparently, they want Dr. Hess Udder Ointment, a concoction created over 100 years ago that makes your hands smooth and feet callus-free. For years, I tried being sensitive, considerate, romantic. This is how little I knew about the opposite sex.

With a name like Udder Ointment, it should either be something you spread over that specific part of the bovine anatomy or, at the very least, it should *come* from the cow's udder. For example: Vegetable oil comes from vegetables and baby oil is for babies. On the other hand, there's Lucas Oil and Olive Oyl. I could make fun of both of those names, but I like my seats on the 40-yard line and I'd never antagonize a woman whose boyfriend has huge forearms.

So how did they come up with this udderly ridiculous name? (I tried to resist that pun, but I am a weak person.) Dr. Hess introduced his original product to turn-of-the-twentieth-century farmers who lamented that their cows' udders were extremely raw and chapped. The fact that the farmers' wives and children were huddled next to the wood-burning stove, withered from the harsh Midwestern blizzards, was of little concern. But those chafed udders? How unsightly. Something needed to be done.

So the farmers applied Dr. Hess' emollient cream to the cows' semi-privates. Soon it was discovered that those doing the milking also benefited. Just what a guy needs when he's tilling his 300 acres of corn: softened hands. Not only that, but after a session in the barn milking Elsie—and shoveling out the manure—farmers found that their silky touch made their wives eager for romance. Dr. Hess was to become a rich man. And a godfather several times over.

The Dr. Hess enterprise was not content with producing only the ointment. They later developed a lip balm called the Udder Stick. Can you think of a product whose name better says: Spread that on my kisser? It's marketing genius.

The company that Dr. Hess founded in 1898 has been in several hands over the years. Those hands were always soft and delicate, but a few of them might have gotten caught in the cookie jar, so now ownership is back in the family, with the founder's great-granddaughter.

In an act of humanitarianism, the newly owned company donates Udder Ointment to our troops in Iraq and Afghanistan. Generations of soldiers have enjoyed care packages from home that included posters of Betty Grable, Farrah Fawcett or Britney Spears. Chocolate also hit the spot. Often, a good cigar was tucked away in a pair of socks. Now imagine the rapture that unfolded when a year's supply of Udder Ointment first hit the runway in Baghdad?

Yes, a product's name can make a big difference in its success. Take toothpaste. Crest, Colgate, and Pepsodent appeal to the woman shopper but have no allure for the typical man. I'd market a dentifrice in the shape of a beer can with a bikini-clad woman on the tube, enticing men to gently squeeze the contents. I'm going to call it Pig Paste. Because I know what men want.

Spreading the News

BOISE, Idaho - Police in Idaho think they might have solved a year-long condiment spree. Authorities say a 74-year-old woman was arrested after pouring mayonnaise in a library book drop box. She may be connected to nine other condiment-related crimes.

The first thing I did when I read this news release was send the Idaho police a thank you note for practically writing my weekly newspaper column for me. You could watch every *Twilight Zone* episode, read every Sherlock Holmes short story ever written and see every Coen Brothers movie and I'm tellin' you, the words "condiment-related crimes" is not going to pop up. This story was a gift from the people of Idaho who gave us the raw materials to make the French fry. Idaho's nickname? The Gem State. Once again, they have delivered. Thank you. And now let's move on . . .

I'm basically an honest person, so I don't spend a lot of time thinking about what I would do if circumstances had led me to a life of crime. However, I've seen enough bad-guy movies to know that when you're looking for shifty ways to make a living, the answer does not lie in a select variety of sauces. I did resist an early influence to be a crook. My mother was an unrepentant

Sweet and Low thief, so I saw firsthand (and with sleight of hand) how easy it was to score big at White Castle or Steak 'n Shake. Mom seemed like a nice person to some people, but those close to her knew that her sweet disposition was artificial.

Apparently, the woman who defiled the books walked around with a backpack that concealed her two sandwich spreads of choice. The police could not legally stop and search her without a warrant or they would have violated her second condiment rights. It's a sad day when it's legal to own an Uzi, but a squeezy bottle of mayonnaise is suspect. The woman accused the police of profiling her, but when you leave a trail of Gulden's Mustard packets behind you, this is considered probable cause. She was also detained at the airport for having more than two ounces of ketchup in her carry-on. The low-life in front of her? Box cutters and a Jim Bowie knife in his raincoat. No problem. Welcome aboard.

I do think that pouring mayo down a book slot at a library is a serious offense, although judges should be able to use discretion in sentencing. Hellmann's on Hemingway is wrong, but Teriyaki on Dostoevsky does have a certain international flavor to it.

This is a bad time for *Law and Order* to go off the air. All their stories are ripped from actual headlines and if we should have, say, a chutney-related murder, I don't trust the people over at *CSI Las Vegas* to take the case seriously.

Other than mayo in the return slot, news sources were reluctant to reveal the other nine condiment capers—for fear, I suppose, that a wave of food-topping, copy-cat crimes would sprinkle the country. There was one leak: The woman did not use Worcestershire Sauce during the commission of any offense. I hope the folks at Lea & Perrins hear about this. When you have a high sodium product, you really need to brag about its low crime rate.

The woman was released, by the way, and put on probation. The judge thought she might be a flight risk, and sure enough, at last report she was on the lam. I hope she had some mint jelly in her purse.

This Bud's for You

When I was about six years old, our family doctor chastised my mother when he discovered that Joan used Q-tips to clean her children's ears. "Never," I remember him saying in the sternest of tones, "put anything in a child's ear smaller than an elbow."

I wish that general admonition had filtered down to little Eric Shoenbaum who, during my first year at summer camp, managed to slam his right elbow into not only my ear, but also my eye, nose and mouth.

Since then I've always taken good care of my ears, but lately they've let me down. Here's the problem: I can't get the earbuds that connect to my iPod to stay in place. I see people jogging, riding their bikes, walking their dogs, even playing Twister while the whole time those little suckers remain neatly wedged in position.

Not for me, they don't. First the right one falls out and dangles alongside my head, then the left one loosens and lands in the hood of my sweatshirt. Often the entire wire gets tangled on my dog's leash or caught in my bicycle chain. Once I leaned over to get a pen out of my glove compartment, hooked the wires on my gear shift and almost strangled myself.

I thought I was alone in my plight but apparently there are others suffering in silence. Literally. According to an article in the *New York Times*, two out of ten people endure a disorder called Earbud Cartilage Deficiency Syndrome, sometimes known as ECDS, but if you're looking for a good laugh at a cocktail party you really need to say all those words out loud.

For every 20 ears out there, four are having a heck of a time keeping it all together. My wife does not have this problem, by the way. She is cartilaginously well-endowed and, I am proud to say, it is all natural.

One techie website reports that people with this problem lack an antitragus in the ear canal, which is "a small tubercle that points anteriorly and is separated from the tragus by the intertragic notch." Sorry to bore you with the obvious.

To combat this abnormality, somebody needs to pay a lot more attention to product specifications. Here's a description of a set of earbuds on eBay: "Full metal housing, cold forged from solid aluminum, anodized finish, with a tactile ID system, flexible joints and a full spectrum of hyper-balanced micro drivers." Am I buying earbuds or a lunar module? I also discovered that earbuds have funny names like M&Ms and strawberry cupcakes. If you told people you were putting M&Ms in your ears, they'd think you weren't eating right.

It's unfortunate that you can't try on earbuds before you buy them, but that would be disgusting, if your selection had been in someone else's canals first. I think about gross stuff like that, which is why I haven't bought a new bathing suit in 20 years.

On one Internet site you can get a fun pack of earbuds in three different sizes for only

$69.95. Okay, some people have two different-sized ears—I get that. But I think the market for three mismatched ears has limited sales potential.

Maybe I should stop obsessing about this. In my senior years, I'm already dealing with failing vision, sinus problems and a receding hairline. I don't need to be distracted by side issues.